THE
COMPLETE
NANNY
GUIDE

THE COMPLETE NANNY GUIDE

Solutions to
Parents' Questions
About Hiring
And Keeping An
In-Home
Caregiver

Cora Hilton Thomas

AVON BOOKS ◆ NEW YORK

THE COMPLETE NANNY GUIDE is an original publication of Avon Books. This edition has never before appeared in book form.

AVON BOOKS
A division of
The Hearst Corporation
1350 Avenue of the Americas
New York, New York 10019

Copyright © 1995 by Cora Hilton Thomas
Inside back cover author photo copyright © 1995 by Glamour Shots
Published by arrangement with the author
Library of Congress Catalog Card Number: 95-1710
ISBN: 0-380-78228-6

Library of Congress Cataloging in Publication Data:

Thomas, Cora Hilton.
   The complete nanny guide : solutions to parents' questions about
hiring and keeping an in-home caregiver / Cora Hilton Thomas.
      p. cm.
Rev. ed. of: Mother's helpmates. 1994.
1. Nannies—United States.   2. Child care—United States.   3. Child care workers—
United States.   I. Thomas, Cora Hilton. Mother's helpmates.   II. Title.
HQ778.63.T48   1995   95-1710
649—dc20   CIP

First Avon Books Trade Printing: September 1995

AVON TRADEMARK REG. U.S. PAT. OFF. AND IN OTHER COUNTRIES, MARCA REGISTRADA,
HECHO EN U.S.A.

Printed in the U.S.A.

OPM   10   9   8   7   6   5   4   3   2   1

This book is dedicated to all children; may it help provide better child care. I also dedicate this book to my own children, Stephen, Alecia, and Ryan, and to my husband, Scott, for all their patience and support while I wrote it, and to the loving memory of my mother, the best mother of all, Cora Mae Chalk Hilton (1930–1976), who taught me the importance of a mother's loving guidance in a child's life.

Acknowledgments

I am grateful for all the help, support, and information I received from many of my clients while writing this book. I am also grateful to Jeff Corydon III; Valerie Hogan for her illustrations; Scott Thomas for his computer training and setup; the Tampa/Hillsborough County library system for assisting with research; and the Criminal Division of the Justice Department in Washington, D.C., and various state law enforcement agencies for their contributions. My thanks to professionals and teachers like Marian Jones at Care Options at the University of South Florida; the National Information Center for Children and Youth with Disabilities; the U.S. Department of Education Office for Civil Rights; the Council for Exceptional Children; United Cerebral Palsy; National Easter Seals Society; and the Child Care Action Campaign.

God bless all the children big and small
for on this earth they have no choice,
they have no voice.

God bless all the children
for the world they see will never be
what it seems to be.

Light their path when the darkness surrounds them.
Give them love,
let it glow all around them.

God bless all the children
shield them from all harm,
keep them safe, keep them warm.

Contents

Contents

List of Appendices

Introduction

Every child deserves the best, most professional care that a mother and father can afford. This book answers parents' most common questions when considering child care. It also provides, in one convenient guide, all the information you need to hire in-home help and will save you the labor and cost of enlisting a child care placement agency. If you are wondering if you can afford a nanny, or about the benefits of hiring a nanny versus taking your child to a day care center, this book will help you and your family make your choice. It offers a detailed outline of the standard procedures a nanny placement agency uses when screening household help for families, and provides information gathered through more than a decade of experience in placing child care helpers with families with all kinds of needs. Even if you are already using an agency, this guide will explain exactly what is involved in hiring household help so that you'll know what you can reasonably expect from the agency and your caregiver.

These pages present the precious information I needed and eventually acquired as a mother, and later used to found my own child care agency, Mother's Helpmates, in 1983. Although my children are now almost grown, I still see a need for quality child care from the parents who call for my help. Nowadays, fifty-one percent of mothers return to work before their child's first birthday. Statistics show that approximately eleven million American children under the age of six need child care either full-time or part-time. With today's rampant fears of child abuse making the search for quality child care more daunting than ever, this book offers a reassuring resource for parents who don't know how to start or where to turn for a helping hand.

In-home Care
Versus
Day Care

Whether you're choosing child care for your first baby or your third child, it's important to assess the pros and cons of your options and, of course, to compare the costs.

Can I Afford a Nanny?

There's no getting around the fact that the average wage for a professional nanny starts at $5 an hour for one child. Weekly salaries generally range from about $200 to $400 a week, which adds up to roughly $10,000 to $20,000 a year. The salary increases with each child and the nanny's level of experience. For day care, the estimated cost for one child is $85 to $100 per week, or roughly $4,500 to $5,000 per year, depending on where you live. On the other hand, if you have more than one child, the cost of day care may double. Parents with three or more children may find that in-home care is actually cheaper than day care.

Parents who hire nannies are responsible not only for the nanny's salary, but also for her social security taxes, federal unemployment tax, and, depending on the laws of the state in which you live, state unemployment tax. Federal and state income taxes are the nanny's responsibility unless other arrangements are made. When considering hiring a nanny, take into account that the time spent keeping proper records can be considerable if you do it yourself.

If the cost of in-home care seems steep, bear in mind that federal income tax deductions you may take for child care will help ease the financial burden. You might also check with your employer about special child care compensation programs. Enrolling in a dependent care flexible spending account program will allow you to set aside untaxed money from your paychecks for child care. Remember, reliable child care usually benefits the employer, since employees are less preoccupied with their children's welfare while at work, and miss fewer days.

Will a Nanny Suit My Needs?

Many two-income families choose to have one-on-one care in their own homes, since many people believe that children develop a sense of security from personal attention in their home environment. Single parents who hold this view may need to work out creative arrangements—such as sharing a nanny (and splitting the salary) with other single parents or a small family.

One of the drawbacks of day care is that most facilities will not keep a sick child. At any sign of illness, they will ask the parent to take the child home. Many parents believe that children in day care also catch more colds and viruses, though some feel this drawback is countered by the positive social skills their children develop in the day care environment.

Here are the most important questions for you and your family to consider before choosing a nanny or a day care center.

1. How much can I afford to pay someone without cutting back on other family activities?

2. Does my work schedule require long hours, overtime, or traveling? Will my work directly affect my child care decision?

3. Does my schedule overlap with my spouse's, or are they identical? How does my spouse's schedule affect our child care needs?

4. Is my schedule flexible enough to accommodate a stop at the day care facility while going to and from work?

5. Can friends or family fill in or help out as needed? What would their help cost if I paid them?

6. Will I lose money if I stay home from work with a sick child? Will I be docked pay or even lose my job?

When making the final decision for child care, be certain that you can afford your choice for at least a year. Make sure your work schedule is adaptable to your child care schedule. If your job requires overtime, enlist an alternate person to pick up your child, such as a family member or close friend with whom your child can stay until you get off work. A word to the wise: personal problems can sometimes arise when child care doesn't work out with family and friends. It's always best to make sure parents' work schedules match the hours of the child care you choose.

What Kind
of Person
Do I Need?

There are many kinds of in-home providers, all of whom use different names and titles. The main ones are listed below, along with their job descriptions. Look them over, and you will probably find the one that best suits your family's needs.

Aide: One who helps or furnishes support or relief for a family. Duties may include helping with laundry, cooking, cleaning, and similar tasks. An aide may have basic medical training, such as a nurse's aide, and may give medication and baths.

Au pair (American style): Usually a young woman (age eighteen to twenty-five) who lives with a family, provides help with household chores, and takes care of the family's children part-time. She usually works

7

under the direction of a parent and may or may not have previous experience.

Au pair (European style):   A European or other foreign national in the United States who performs domestic work and cares for children in exchange for room and board, spending money, and the chance to learn a family's language and customs. She lives with the host family and receives a salary. Such individuals are not always experienced in child care or familiar with American children's needs.

Baby-sitter: One who cares for babies or young children when the parents or family aren't home.

Caregiver: A person who assists a sick or disabled child but does not have formal medical training.

Governess: Traditionally, an educationally qualified person employed by a family for the full-time or part-time education of school-age children. She is not usually assigned either domestic work or the physical care of small children. Sometimes a governess is employed to travel with a family and educate or train children on the move.

Helpmate (mother's helper):   A helper who assists parents and acts as an extension of the mother in performing the duties of the home and caring for the family's children. The helper may live in or outside the family home.

Housekeeper: One employed to perform or direct housekeeping. Duties can include doing laundry, vacuuming, dusting, cleaning windows and floors, and the like.

Live-in: Someone who resides at the place of employment, such as a nanny or other caregiver hired to care for children. In general, the advantage of employing a live-in is having help available if needed with the children, although most nannies prefer a set work schedule whether or not they live with the family. The disadvantage is the extra cost of room and board, utilities and food, and the loss of privacy.

Nanny: A child's nurse, employed by a family on either a live-in or a live-out basis exclusively for child care and related domestic tasks. Nannies work variable hours and are usually given almost total authority in areas outlined by the family.

A nanny usually manages the children's activities and outings, intellectual stimulation, language training, transportation, discipline, and any child-related housekeeping duties, such as taking care of the child's food preparation, laundry, bathing, and supervising homework. The nanny must be able to communicate effectively with both parents and the children.

Nannies may be any age from eighteen to sixty or more. They should have a high school education or the equivalent and solid character references. They should be in good health, with up-to-date documentary proof of immunization and a negative TB test. Genuine love and respect for children is a must.

Nannies can generally be classified in three categories:

1. Single young women with day care or baby-sitting experience. They usually want to work with children for a year or longer and may have had prior child care jobs. They want to

work closely with children for the satisfaction of giving one-on-one care.

2. Older and more mature women who have raised families and are drawn to in-home day care based on their past experience with children.

3. Women with a degree or educational background relating to children who want to work with a family to supplement classroom learning.

Nurse's aide: One who provides private medical care for a child.

Visiting nurse: A registered nurse employed by a public health agency or hospital to promote community health, especially by visiting and treating sick people in their homes. A nurse may be hired by a family to provide private care for a child.

How Do I Decide Which Kind of Helper Is Best for Me?

First, prepare a realistic list of your family's needs. You must determine not only what the job will involve, but when and how many hours you will need someone to work. Match your requirements as closely as possible to one of the job descriptions above.

For example, if you're a mother who stays at home but needs additional help, you may want a mother's helper. If you have to leave home regularly for short periods and just need someone to watch your child, a baby-sitter will probably suit your needs. While some parents will only accept a trained nanny, many sitters are experienced and well-qualified to care for your children. A lot of caring people who love children find fulfillment as sitters.

Don't search for a nanny if you really need someone to help you run your household. Nannies who are trained for positions in child care simply won't want a housekeeping job, and a housekeeper will not be as adept at child care as a nanny. As training schools for nannies are becoming ever more popular, nannies are increasingly setting basic standards for their jobs that apply across their field.

How Much Will
Help Cost?

Now that you've determined what kind of help you
need, the next step is reconciling your needs with
your means. Salary depends on the job to be done
and the amount of experience an applicant has. For
nannies and sitters, the average hourly wages vary
between $5 and $10 in most states. (Minimum wage
is currently $4.25 per hour, which provides an annual
wage about $4,000 below the poverty level.) To deter-
mine how much you'll need to pay in-home help,
you need to consider the cost of living in your area.
For example, wages are generally higher in Boston
than in Tampa. The most obvious way to figure out
the market rate is to ask someone who currently em-
ploys a nanny or sitter. You can also call a few of

the child care placement agencies listed in the yellow pages under child care (or in Appendix G in this book). When asking about wages, be sure to give a thorough description of the job to be done.

If you are serious about hiring someone, don't offer low-end wages. I often hear complaints from nannies who have been offered ridiculously low pay. It's important to make absolutely sure that you can afford a nanny's salary before you advertise for one. You don't want to go to the trouble to advertise only to discover that the going rate is more than you can afford.

If you find an applicant who asks for a very small salary, be suspicious. The sitter may have a criminal record and hope that unsuspecting parents will be in such a hurry to find a nanny that they will overlook the details, or that parents who can ill-afford a high salary may think a nanny who accepts a pittance is a good deal. This could spell trouble. Your child's safety may be at risk.

It's also best to beware of any household employee who requests to work for cash only. Such an arrangement sounds easy but can lead to trouble. If you do not withhold the proper taxes from an employee's salary, and the employee later seeks benefits, such as worker's compensation or social security from the government, she might be caught and charged with fraud. This will also put you in a sticky situation. Not long ago, my referral service was asked to appear in court to testify in a case concerning a nanny who collected benefits from the government but had not reported all her earnings. It's best to protect yourself from anyone who appears to be trying to cheat the government. You don't want to end up in court or to be audited by the IRS. When you hire someone,

always make sure everything is in writing to mini-
mize the chances of misunderstandings about salary
and duties.

Here are some tips about specific pay situations:

Au pair: Salary is usually reduced to compensate
for the au pair's room and board supplied by the
family. The Clinton Administration passed a new
regulation in early 1995 stipulating that the minimum
au pair salary is $115 per week. This regulation in-
cludes the cost of $500 for training the au pair in
child care.

Live-in: The weekly salary should include any expenses for utilities and food.

Sharing a nanny: Some nannies work for several
families on a short-term basis, taking job leads from
referral and home health agencies. Their weekly salary is usually split among the employing families.
The hourly rate for such a nanny may be a little
higher, to compensate for the strain of caring for
more than one child at more than one house.

Housekeeper: Salaries are usually $10 an hour, since
housekeepers are usually needed only once or twice
a week for heavy cleaning. If the employee is also a
nanny or sitter, the hourly rate will range from $5 to
$10 an hour, since nannies are only expected to pick
up after the children.

Holiday and vacation pay: These benefits should
be discussed in advance with your nanny. It's only
fair that parents who receive holiday and vacation
pay themselves should offer these benefits to their
nanny. The nanny can take her vacation during the

same holidays and vacation periods as the family. (Some families may want to require a probation period before offering such benefits.)

Health insurance: Families that can afford it may offer insurance for their employee, although most families will probably feel they can't afford it.

Where Do I
Find a Nanny?

Once you've determined what kind of in-home help you need and how much you can pay, there are several options for locating prospective employees. The cheapest way is to post advertisements in strategic locations in your community. If you don't have the time to conduct your own advertising campaign and can afford to pay a fee, a child care placement agency will apply specialized expertise to finding a nanny for you (see Chapter 10 for more details on choosing an agency, fees, and services).

Where Do I Advertise?

Rather than advertising in the major *newspapers*, which can be expensive, place ads in the *community shopper guides*. Smaller community papers offer cheaper advertising and will yield applicants who live in your community. Call your *church and community services organization* and ask if they have bulletin boards for posting help-wanted ads. Most *YMCAs* also have a child care referral service for parents who are looking for sitters, nanny placement services, private in-home day care, and day care centers in a given community. You can also go to any *community college* in your area and place your ad on the bulletin boards for job-seeking students. Try to place some ads near the school's early childhood education department; students there are perfect child care candidates. Look in the yellow pages for any *nanny schools* (and check the list of nanny schools in Appendix A). Nannies and au pairs who are finished with their training will be looking for work. If you do not find any nanny schools in the yellow pages, call your library for listings in your area. *Radio stations* often offer community service announcements, so why not ask the station to announce your job? *Nursing schools* are full of students studying pediatric nursing, or certified nursing assistants who are looking for work. These women are trained and qualified to help families with normal children as well as children with special needs and disabled persons. Nursing schools are also a good resource for CPR classes, in case you want your sitter or nanny to be certified in CPR or first aid.

Another source for child care applicants is your local *senior neighbors services* organization. Senior citizens can offer good care for a sick loved one or a disabled child, and can often use the extra income. Bear in mind, however, that some senior citizens may not feel they have the energy to handle toddlers, though it will depend on the individual. If you have a swimming pool, make sure that any person you hire is not afraid of water and can swim, in case of an emergency. Be sure to include any pertinent information about pets, a pool, and so forth, as well as the job you're offering.

What Should My Ad Say?

No matter which route you choose, you will need to develop an accurate job description. Here's an outline of the things to mention when putting your ad together:

- A concise description of job duties.
- The location of the job.
- Weekly salary or hourly rate.
- Days of the week you need someone to work.
- Experience or special training needed.
- Transportation needed or available.

In general, pets should be mentioned in your advertisement, in case applicants have allergies or a fear of dogs or other animals. Be sure to mention any unusual pets, such as snakes.

The most effective ads are short and specific. When putting an ad together for a bulletin board, make it colorful to help attract attention.

Here are some sample ads:

Here is a sample cover letter and ad that can be sent or faxed to the student affairs office at a local college:

ATTENTION: Student services/John Smith
             Jane Hill Campus
             Fax. no 555–4444

FROM: Mary Jo Thomas, 555–3333
             Fax no. 555–1234

Mr. Smith, here is a job bulletin to post at the school for the child care position we discussed last Friday. If you or any applicants have questions, please call 555–3333. Thank you for your help.

                            Sincerely,
                            Mrs. Thomas

ATTENTION:

Mary Jo Thomas is looking for a loving
nanny for her two children for after
school, Monday–Friday. Pay is $5.25/
hr. plus mileage. Hours are 2 to 7 P.M.
Duties include: picking up the children
from school, some light
housekeeping, preparing meals for
children. Applicants must have
experience/references/reliable
transportation/home phone.
If interested, please call 555–3333
or fax resumé to 555-1234

5

How Do I Conduct an Interview?

How Long Will It Take to Find a Nanny?

Once you've created a job description and posted an ad, take the time to find the right person, and don't be rushed. Allow a minimum of two to three weeks to interview and screen your prospects. The amount of time it will take to find someone who fits your needs will also depend to some extent on the work hours and the job requirements. If the requirements are complicated or out of the ordinary, you'll need to

23

allow a bit more time to find someone with relevant experience. The time it will take to hire someone will also depend on what you will pay. If you offer what the job is worth, you probably won't have to wait long for the right person.

What Basic Information Should I Request in an Interview?

It's important to be thorough and methodical when interviewing prospective helpers. Checking all references and past work history carefully will go a long way toward preventing frequent turnover in your household personnel.

What Information Should I Request from the Applicant?

When considering an applicant for a job in your home, ask for the following:

1. Birth certificate
2. Social security card
3. Valid driver's license
4. A home phone number
5. Proof of a physical exam within the past two years
6. Work references with addresses and phone numbers for the past three years
7. Character references with addresses and phone numbers

8. Neighbor references and phone numbers

9. CPR certificate

You may want to ask the applicants to make copies of these items and any other types of certification they have and bring them to the final interview. If you need someone with special training in caring for children with special needs, this is especially important.

You can use the sample application form in Appendix B1 and the screening sheet in Appendix B2 as part of your interview. Make sure that the application sheet is filled out completely and signed. (Always be sure to get the applicant's signature giving consent to verify her previous employment and any of the other information she provides.) If you interview the applicant verbally, don't skip over any important questions, and keep close track of her answers. Review important information once more before the applicant leaves. When hiring someone, keep copies of her social security card, birth certificate, driver's license, and CPR certificate in a file.

Where Should I Conduct the Interview?

Over the course of my career as a child care placement specialist, I've found it enormously important to interview both sitters and parents in their own homes before making any final decision on placement. The technique of in-home interviewing helps to determine the character of the applicants and those who live with them. My aim is to match the personalities of family and sitter. I can't risk placing a criminal or a potential child abuser or anyone who lives with such a person.

Interviewing a nanny at her home gives you a chance to get to know her in her own setting. Many people feel more at ease during an interview at home. You can sometimes narrow down the applicants for a nanny position just by mentioning the in-home interview. Any applicants who have something to hide will change their mind about applying then and there. If you feel apprehensive about going alone to an interview at someone's home before having met the person, ask the applicant to come to a restaurant or another public place the first time. After narrowing the field, you can meet the best prospects at their homes before making a final decision. Remember, the person you're seeking will be working in your home without any supervision. For this reason, I recommend interviewing any applicant you're seriously considering at least twice.

For the second visit, ask the applicant to come to your house for the interview. Have your children present to see her reaction to them and vice versa. It's important to allow prospective helpers to spend some time with your children to ascertain how they get along before you make a decision about hiring anyone. Some caregivers, although experienced, may not be compatible with your children, since children have their own personalities and preferences at an early age. Remember, if your child isn't happy, you won't be either.

What Should I Look for During an Interview?

During the interview, notice whether the nanny acknowledges or speaks to the children. Discuss your ideas for child rearing and discipline and hers. Pay attention to her questions, as well as her answers. Make it clear that she should never discipline your children physically. Ask the applicant how she would deal with a temper tantrum and how she would handle specific emergencies, such as choking, minor injuries, or fire.

The applicant's appearance is always important. If a nanny or sitter doesn't look clean and neat before she works for you, she isn't likely to improve after being hired. The interview is the time to make judgments concerning appearance and personal hygiene. After all, the person caring for your children will be responsible for keeping them clean and preparing their food.

When making a final decision, review each applicant's character references and comments, and consider her lifestyle. Don't hire someone whose approach to child rearing or whose morals conflict with yours, only to dismiss her a little later. Nannies are not going to change their beliefs, personal philosophy, or way of life for a job. The time to find out about these important issues is before, not after, you hire your nanny.

Here are a few more things to explore: Does she have a fiancee or husband? Do they have children? Who will stay home and take care of her children when they are sick? If they don't have children, how soon do they plan to start a family? Find out if your applicant is a student in school or is planning to go back to school in the future. It's best not to hire a student who plans to return to school after only a short time on the job. Her school schedule may interfere with your working hours, forcing you to replace her sooner or later. Will she be taking days off for particular religious holidays or other obligations? If you want a nanny to stay with your family, don't hire one who has jumped from job to job. Chances are good that such a nanny will not be with you for long. Also if a nanny has traveled a lot, there is less chance of her staying with you. A local nanny is generally a better choice because it's more likely that she wants to stay in the area.

There are several important things to consider when hiring a nanny. While older nannies have more experience, they may also tend to have more difficulty taking instructions sometimes, especially if they have raised children of their own. Many don't feel it necessary to know how to swim or how to perform CPR, which can be a problem given that most children love water, whether they can swim or not, and they can easily fall in. If you have a pool and the nanny is afraid of the water or can't swim, I can't recommend that you employ her. Even children who know how to swim may have accidents and need help.

Make sure to ask every applicant the questions in this chapter and to take careful note of the responses. A parent must feel comfortable about leaving a nanny in charge of household and children. To avoid problems in the future, explore the nanny's attitudes toward her job when you interview her, and save the trouble of replacing her later.

Should you find a person you like who wants to start work earlier than you need someone, offer part-time work until you are ready for a full-time helper. This will give you and your helper a chance to ease the children into a new situation more smoothly.

What Should I Say About the Salary?

When you interview a nanny, it is your obligation to make sure that you discuss the exact amount of her salary after taxes are withheld, since you will need to factor unemployment taxes and other payroll deductions into her gross salary. (We will discuss withholding taxes in Chapter 8.) It's also important

Ten Red Flags That Often Signal Trouble in an Interview

1. Applicant refuses to give home phone number and doesn't have numbers for work references or neighbor references.

2. Applicant refuses an in-home interview.

3. Applicant refuses to give valid ID or driver's license number, or to provide social security card.

4. Applicant refuses to sign a release for a criminal background check.

5. Applicant does not interact very well with the child to be cared for.

6. Applicant has had a lot of short-term jobs, which may indicate the applicant may not be reliable and dependable, and may not do a good job.

7. Applicant has moved around a lot, which may indicate she is running from trouble or trying to keep from getting caught.

8. Applicant requests very low pay, which may be trying to hide a lack of experience or other faults.

9. Applicant has a number of traffic tickets and will be driving.

10. Applicant is overqualified for position and pay.

Top Ten Tips

1. Your nanny must interact well with both child and parents.

2. Your hours of need should match the hours that the caregiver is available.

3. Your nanny must have reliable transportation to and from work.

4. You should have the same ideas about discipline as the caregiver.

5. Your nanny must be reliable in an emergency, especially if you have a child with a disability or special needs.

6. You should feel welcome to spend time with your nanny while she is minding your child at any time.

7. You should know your nanny's reasons for wanting the job.

8. The applicant should not be looking for just temporary employment.

9. Your nanny should not be accepting less money than she will need to live comfortably (or you will find yourself looking for a nanny all over again).

10. You should interview any nanny you are serious about at least twice before making a decision, and at least one interview should take place in caregiver's home if she is to come to your home to work.

to discuss what benefits you can and can't offer. If a nanny wants to be paid in cash, make sure that she understands that she will be responsible for paying her own taxes, assuming that she is self-employed.

How Do I
Screen
Household
Help?

While it is important for any employer to screen prospective employees, it is imperative when that employee is going to provide child care in your home, in many cases without supervision. This chapter addresses the details of the screening process.

It's usually best to screen the applicant after the second interview or as soon as you are sure you are comfortable with her. Bear in mind that to screen an applicant properly, you will need the full cooperation of your potential nanny or housekeeper. If possible, have the applicant sign a form releasing all information regarding past work history for your use. You'll find a sample form in Appendix C1.

The following are some areas to scrutinize when screening employees yourself:

Past employment history. Noting the duration of the applicant's last few jobs can help you assess the amount of commitment she has. If past jobs were mostly short-term, find out why. Did the employer move, or was the applicant hired for only a short period? Ask the applicant for the phone numbers and addresses of the previous employers and call them to check the references. Ask what duties the nanny performed for them. Ask if the applicant is reliable, punctual, and honest. Ask if they think the nanny can perform the duties you desire. For a more detailed response, you can also write for further information using the performance request form in Appendix C2.

Character references. You can check an applicant's character references by calling the parties listed by the applicant and asking the questions provided on the performance request form in Appendix C1, or sending the form by mail and requesting a response.

Check on education and training. Some applicants will give a list of special training to impress you with their qualifications. You may want to verify such information, especially if this special training is, in fact, necessary to the care of your child. You'll need the name and address of schools the applicant claims to have attended so you can call and query these schools. Also check with the state to verify any nursing or nursing assistant certifications. Nannies and sitters do not typically have a lot of education or job experience except in child care. The only qualifications a nanny really needs are good character and lots of love for children.

Physical exam or drug testing. The applicant should have had a recent physical exam (within the past two years). It's best to make sure that you have someone who is healthy enough to care for your child, and that the applicant is not taking any drugs or medications that will hinder her ability to care for your child. A physical exam is also a way to check for drug abuse. If you set up an examination with your family doctor, or a doctor's walk-in clinic, you should pay for all costs. Again, you'll need to get the applicant's permission in writing to receive the results of the examination.

Criminal background.   When you are serious about an applicant, you will want to check for any criminal background. It may be easiest to ask the applicant to obtain a copy of her own record for you or have her request that one be sent to you. If the applicant has had a number of jobs outside your state, you will probably want a paralegal or detective agency to do the screening, since agencies have easy access to information that private individuals cannot obtain without tedious and time-consuming labor. You will find phone numbers for agencies and other types of services in the yellow pages. Before you start your background check, be sure to get a release form signed by the applicant that authorizes you to query the appropriate authorities. (See Criminal Background Release Form in Appendix C3.)

Although it's not easy to conduct the checks by yourself, it can save you some money if you have the time to do it. To do it yourself, write to the FBI's Identification Department in Washington, D.C., or call 202–324–5278. They can direct you to the agency in your state that will provide criminal background information on caregivers. When calling the FBI, explain why you are asking for such criminal back-ground data. Tell them you want to protect your child from any criminal or child abuser. They will be glad to help you contact the proper agency.

Abuse registries in many states record complaint reports of child abuse. The National Child Protection Act of 1993 (Public Law 103–209, effective December 20, 1993) makes it easier to keep track of child abus-ers all over the country. The law requires each state to report all child abuse information to a national child abuse records system established in Washing-ton, D.C.

Each state is also empowered to pass legislation that requires employers and agencies to contact a state agency and request a nationwide background check for the purpose of determining whether a pro-vider has been convicted of a crime that bears upon fitness for the responsibility for the safety and well-being of children. The state agency can access and review state and federal criminal history through the national criminal history background check system and make reasonable efforts to respond to any in-quiry within fifteen business days.

The child care abuse information reported by each state will contain the following facts on persons who have been arrested for or convicted of any child abuse crime: full name, race, sex, date of birth, height, weight, fingerprints, a brief description of the child abuse crime or offenses for which the person has been arrested or convicted, the disposition of the charge, and any other information that the attorney general deems useful in identifying persons arrested for or convicted of a child abuse crime.

For more complete information on the National Child Protection Act, contact:

Federal Bureau of Investigation
National Crime Information Center
Tenth Street and Pennsylvania Avenue, N.W.
Washington, DC 20535

See Appendix C4 for a list of various state agencies throughout the country that can help you obtain criminal background information. Again, before you start this process by yourself, bear in mind that it will take time and at least a few long-distance phone calls to get the information you need, especially if the nanny or caregiver has lived in several states.

Driving record.   If driving your children to and from school or other activities is part of your job description, you will want to check an applicant's driving record to see if she has any history of driving infractions. You should know about any past DUI (driving under the influence of alcohol) violations, speeding tickets, or accidents. You may make your request in person or write to your department of motor vehicles. In most states you can also call the highway patrol for such information. The cost for obtaining this driving record is between $3 and $5 for the first page, with each additional page usually costing $1. To get a copy of someone's driving record, you'll need to provide the following identification data: full name, all residences during past years, date of birth, driver's license number, and social security number. When requesting the record by mail, you'll need to send the identifying data to the department of motor vehicles or the clerk of the circuit court and specifically request the applicant's driving record. You can also call for a request form, which they will send for you to fill out and return. A notarized letter explaining why you are requesting the driving record may also be helpful (if you don't know where to find a notary, look in your yellow pages or call your local library). Don't forget to include any fees that are applicable.

Credit report.   You might also want to check an applicant's credit to see whether she has any history of writing bad checks or any addresses besides those listed on the application. While most families won't care whether the employee has good credit, this check is just another precautionary step aimed at protecting your home and child from a potential thief. To conduct a credit check, you will need to contact a preemployment screening agency, private investigator, or paralegal. The applicant must also sign a release form giving her permission for the check.

How Do I Keep My Nanny When I've Found the Right One?

The question I am most often asked after placing a nanny is: How can I make her stay with my family forever? The answer is obvious when you consider that most parents expect their nanny or sitter to do everything—but they also expect to pay a minimum wage. Of course, some parents cannot afford to pay much, especially single parents. I find it ironic, however, that families with lower incomes usually offer to pay their nanny the highest wages. In my experience, families that have more to offer are not always fair when deciding a salary. Ask yourself: Would I do this job for this amount of money? If your answer is no, then reconsider. After all, if you won't do it, what makes you think someone else will? When you start interviewing applicants, you will find that nannies and helpmates are looking for better paying jobs than in the past. Few nannies are going to stay long on a job that pays $4 or $5 an hour if they hear that someone else is paying more for similar work.

Competitive Pay

The more competitive the pay you offer, the longer a nanny will stay. Before I place a nanny in a home, I look at the family's past history with nannies. Families that offer low pay and treat their nannies poorly have a high turnover. If you want a nanny to stay, look carefully at what you are offering. Do you offer the market rate of pay for the area where you live? Does her salary reflect her experience in child care? Do you offer special benefits? Never offer a low rate if you are serious about finding and keeping a nanny.

Benefits

An educated nanny will want top salary and will look for a family that offers this pay. However, some nannies in urgent need of a job may accept a smaller salary when offered such extras as room and board or the use of a vehicle. In some cases, you might want to offer a nanny such compensation along with a lower salary. Allowing a nanny to live in during the work week will save her the cost of transportation to and from her job. A lower salary may be easier to negotiate if her outside expenses can be cut.

Days Off

It's also important to give your nanny at least two days of recuperation a week, and to respect her days off. Don't think that because you have a live-in, she is always at your beck and call. Some families that hire live-ins seem to have the misconception that their nanny should work twenty-four hours a day for eight hours' pay. A sure way to lose a nanny is not to allow her enough free time. Besides, your nanny will do a better job when she gets sufficient rest.

Work Shifts and Overtime

A new mother who has had a caesarean, or who has a colicky baby, may need a nanny around the clock. The best solution is to schedule more than one nanny to give each one some time off. The work hours for any live-in should stay as close to a permanent schedule as possible. This will enable her to schedule her own activities and take care of personal business.

Live-in nannies are the hardest to keep because they usually don't get enough time off. They burn out fast and quit. Parents who work long hours may request a live-in because of their erratic schedules. However, when this is the case, there should be more than one caregiver. Overtime is another problem. Compensate your nanny for any time worked beyond normal duty hours. Do not expect her to work extra hours without reward. Nannies realize there are times when you need them for overtime work, but they also deserve appreciation for their extra efforts. Lack of appreciation is another complaint often heard from sitters who are quitting. If they do their job well or go out of their way for you, show your appreciation by thanking them warmly at the least. Remember, your nanny takes care of the most important members of your family.

Prompt Pay and Amenities

Always pay your helper as promised; don't be late with pay. She needs money for her bills just as you do for yours.

It's also important to make sure your nanny's surroundings are comfortable. If you need a live-in, provide adequate accommodations, including a private bathroom and bedroom. Ask yourself if you would be comfortable in her position. You should feel good about the surroundings you offer her to work in.

Respect

Not being respected is another complaint of unhappy nannies. Don't treat your nanny as if she's beneath you. Treat her with the respect you yourself would want.

Communication

Good communication will also help build a lasting relationship with your nanny or caregiver. Be sure to explain in detail what her duties are and what you expect of her. *Don't ever assume that the nanny already knows what you expect her to do!* Make a list of your instructions to avoid misunderstandings, but don't put so much on the list that it's impossible to get everything done on time. Parents often complain that their nanny isn't doing what they want. Most of the time the problem is that she doesn't have a clue as to what they want. When this happens, it's time for the nanny and parents to sit down and talk and to make that list if they haven't already. (See Appendix D1 for a sample weekly schedule.)

It is usually a good idea to put together your own parent and nanny contract. It should include the basic duties you and the nanny have agreed she will perform, as well as the payment arrangement you have worked out and any other important details. (See Appendix D2 for a sample contract.)

Don't assume that a nanny will do a job the same way you do. There is more than one way to clean and still get the job done. Some parents say: "I'm

Nanny's Bill of Rights

Nannies have the right to expect and be given the following:

1. Two days off each week.
2. Prompt paychecks and paid overtime.
3. Holiday and vacation pay.
4. Respect from children.
5. Clear communication from parents.
6. Support and understanding from parents.
7. Love from family.
8. Raises in pay.
9. Appreciation.
10. Rewards.

paying her to do things my way." Wrong! Try to compromise. What difference does it make *how* it's done as long as the job *is* done?

Finally, don't compare your present nanny to a previous one. The new nanny doesn't want to hear that she will never take the place of the last one. No two people and nannies are ever alike. Discuss your own ideas on child rearing and discipline with her and compare your own similarities and differences, but not those of other nannies.

Taxes,
Social Security,
and
Payroll Programs

When you hire domestic help, you have to comply with certain tax laws. This chapter outlines your main tax responsibilities to the U.S. Government as an employer, including social security taxes, unemployment taxes, and payroll arrangements for your household employee. As you may have heard, even prominent U.S. government officials have failed to pay social security taxes for their employees and incurred heavy penalties as a result. Don't let ignorance cause similar problems for you. It's imperative that parents know the tax responsibilities they assume by employing domestic help. This chapter outlines the major federal tax laws. Be sure to consult with a tax specialist regarding any state laws that may apply to you. It is not mandatory to with hold federal and state income tax from your nanny's salary.

You should always keep all records on your employees and payments related to them for at least three years. Here are the main items you need to keep:

1. Employee's name and social security number.
2. Employee's address and zip code.
3. Wages paid each week to your employee.
4. The total of hours worked each week by your employee, including overtime.
5. A record of any money paid to your employee for room and board, or any money spent on behalf of your live-in or live-out help.

The one case in which you are not responsible for any taxes is when you hire a nanny who proclaims herself self-employed. Some nannies and baby-sitters may claim to be self-employed if they work for more than one family. You may want to offer an independent contract to a nanny in this situation.

The following pages outline the different forms you'll need for your employee's social security taxes and your child care tax deductions. To confirm your tax responsibilities it's always best to call a tax specialist, who can also offer options on deductions concerning child care.

Form SS-4—Application for
Employer Identification Number

Once you decide to hire someone, this is the first form you will need to fill out and submit. If the employee has no social security number, she should apply to the Social Security Administration for one. (See Appendix E1.)

Form W-2—Wage and Tax Statement

The statement of earnings and withholdings must be filed annually for many household employees. It must be given to the employee by January 31 of the following year and transmitted to the Social Security Administration by March 1. (See Appendix E2.)

Form W-4—Employee's
Withholding Allowance Certificate

The purpose of this form is to allow the employer to withhold the correct amount of federal income tax from an employee's wages. You do not have to withhold income taxes for household employees. However, if the employee requests, you may voluntarily do so, in which case you use a Form W-4. (See Appendix E3.)

Form W-5—Earned Income Credit Advance
Payment Certificate

This form is used when an employee is eligible to get a portion of earned income credit in advance along with wages. Employers must make advance payments of this credit to eligible employees who have completed this form. (See Appendix E4.)

Form 942—Employer's Quarterly Tax Return for Household Employees

Filed each quarter of the year, this form covers an employee's social security and Medicare taxes, federal income tax, and advance earned income credit. As of 1995, employers with one in-home employee have the option to file quarterly or on their annual return. Employers with more than one domestic employee must file quarterly. (See Appendix E5.)

Sample—taxes deducted from nanny's gross salary of $200 per week:

Social Security	$200 × 6.2% =	$12.40
Medicare	$200 × 1.45% =	$ 2.90
Total taxes deducted from gross salary		$15.30

Taxes paid by employer:

Social Security	$200 × 6.2% =	$12.40
Medicare	$200 × 1.45% =	$ 2.90
Federal Unemployment Tax	$200 × 6.2% =	$12.40
Florida* State Unemployment Tax	$200 × 2.7% =	$ 5.40
Total taxes paid by employer in addition to nanny's salary		$33.10

The employer will pay a total of $233.10 per week for a nanny's salary of $200 per week. (See the Employee Social Security and Medicare Tax Deduction Table in Appendix E6.)

---

*Varies from state to state, the yearly salary of the employee, and the length of time the employer has been paying unemployment tax.

Form 940-EZ—and 940 Employer's Annual Federal Unemployment (FUTA) Tax Return

This form must be filed each year by all employers before January 31 of the following year. The required payments are made with Form 8109 (federal tax deposit coupons), which you will receive after you apply for an employer ID number. (See Appendices E7 and E8.)

Child Care Tax Deductions

Form 2441, child and dependent care credit on your federal income tax, can be as much as $400 for one child and $960 for two or more. Your credit decreases as family income increases beyond $10,000. For further information, contact the Internal Revenue Service. (See Appendix E9.)

Form 1099—Miscellaneous Income

Parents must give this form to any nanny declaring herself an independent contractor by January 31 to report the previous year's income. It applies to any income totalling at least $600. The employer must also file the form with the IRS. Be aware that, according to current tax law, anyone who classifies an employee as an independent contractor and has no reasonable basis for doing so can be held liable for the employee's unemployment, social security, and Medicare taxes. (See Appendix E10.)

State Taxes

To find out about applicable taxes in your state, call the IRS at 1–800–829–3676 for a referral to the appropriate state bureau in your area. It's also best to talk to a tax specialist.

Now that we have discussed your tax responsibilities as an employer, the next matter is how you actually pay your employee. You can hire a payroll company or accountant to keep track of all your tax responsibilities and distribute paychecks to the employee, if you wish and can afford the fee. Another alternative is to purchase a computer program that calculates federal income taxes, state and local taxes, social security taxes, and federal and state unemployment taxes.

On the opposite page, you'll find an example of a payroll-type check for an employee. The employee's tax withholdings are calculated and printed for each pay period, and the checks come ready to issue to the employee once the employer endorses them. My own child care placement agency, Mother's Helpmates, offers this special payroll service to our clients. If you want more details, contact us at 813–681–5183.

COMPANY NAME
Address
City, State Zip Code

BANK NAME
Branch Office
City, State Zip Code
00–6789/0000

Date _____

PAY TO THE
ORDER OF _____ Employee Name _____ $*********2,742.79

Two Thousand Seven Hundred Forty-Two and 79/100 *** DOLLARS

Employee Name
Address
City, State Zip Code

MEMO _____

- -

COMPANY NAME
Employee Name

	Date	
Payroll: Gross	$13269.21	$3,750.00
(Payroll-FWH)	$ 2142.00	$ -599.00
(Payroll-SWHCA)	$ 492.42	$ -121.33
(Payroll-FICA)	$ 822.69	$ -232.50
(Payroll-MCARE)	$ 192.40	$ -54.38
Total Hours	160.00	
		$2,742.79

YTD Gross Wages
YTD Federal Tax
YTD State Tax
YTD Social Security
YTD Medicare
Total Hours

9

Laws on Hiring In-home Help

When you become an employer of household help, you will have to comply with federal and state laws. Here are the most important ones:

- Federal Fair Labor Standards Act. This act guarantees employees a minimum hourly wage. For domestic service workers, the minimum is currently $4.25 an hour. Full-time baby-sitters employed over twenty hours must be paid minimum wage (W H Publication 1382). Since the federal law is subject to change, it's always best to request an up-to-date copy. You can obtain one through your local library or by calling the labor board in your state.

A regulation passed by the Clinton Administration stipulates that au pairs must have at least six months' experience or training in infant care, and bars them from caring for children under three months old. It also requires au pairs to take at least six hours of college credit courses; families employing au pairs must pay up to $500 for her education.

- Employment Eligibility Verification. A 1986 federal law requires any employer to (1) check each worker's documents proving identity and eligibility to work, (2) have each worker complete part of Form I-9, which contains an attestation that the employer has seen the employee's green card, passport, or other documents, and (3) keep the completed Form I-9 on hand for at least three years, and present it to government officials upon request. (See Appendix F.)

- Immigration Reform and Control Act of 1986. This act stipulates that you should hire only American citizens or those who are authorized to work in the United States.

For more information on these and other laws, call the Justice Department at 202–514–2000, 202–514–4330, or 202–324–5074.

Most states don't require a nanny or household helper to be licensed, but some do. Be sure you know about any state regulations before you hire someone for your home. To find out whether there are special laws for nannies in your state, call the state's law enforcement department. You can also get such information from your city or county licensing department. Don't risk violating any laws.

Using a
Placement
Agency

A child care placement agency will apply specialized experience and expertise to help you in your
search for the right employee. Every agency has a
network of candidates you could not turn up on your
own. If you can afford an agency's commission, you
will save most of the considerable time it takes to
screen prospective caregivers by yourself.

Agencies exist on the fees they charge for their services, which vary from state to state and city to city,
and range from $350 to $4,000. The differences in fees
are based partly on whether a referral or placement
service guarantees placement for sixty days or up to
four years, and on the specific needs of the client.
An agency that charges $4,000 will usually give a
permanent replacement guarantee, however. Some

agencies charge according to your specific need, such as whether you are looking for a live-in or live-out caregiver. Charges may also be based on whether a person needs only a one-day replacement or week-end help. If you hire someone for a few days, you might pay the nanny her fee and the agency for the referral, which will cost anywhere from $10 to $15 for each day you use the nanny. Some agencies will screen someone for a small charge whether or not you employ the applicant, while others will not do spot screening at all.

Check around and find out what is offered in your area. If you can't afford the whole placement fee at once, ask whether you can pay in installments. While most agencies want to be paid promptly at the usual rates, they may be willing to work out a placement fee and terms that you can afford if you ask.

Baby-sitting agencies tend to charge higher hourly rates and take their fee from this money. The family may be asked to pay the sitter a few extra dollars a day for car expenses.

If you decide to use au pair services, you will pay a larger placement fee than you would for a nanny, but the weekly salary for your au pair will usually be lower. Make sure au pairs have been screened properly by the agency. If the au pair is a foreigner, it's worth learning something about the culture of the country she is from, since it's possible that you could wind up with a person whose cultural background doesn't agree with yours.

In general, you get what you pay for, as the old saying goes. So contact your local agencies and ask about their costs and what you'll get for your money. You'll find a list of agencies in Appendix G.

Here are some of the things to look for in choosing an agency:

1. Make sure the agency is licensed. How long have they been in business? Call your state licensing department for more information.

2. Ask for references from past clients. Bear in mind that some agencies may not give out clients' phone numbers or addresses without first getting their permission.

3. Clarify how long the agency's placement guarantee will last. Most agencies offer sixty- to ninety-day placement guarantees.

4. Find out what kind of screening methods the service uses. Agencies should be using the following screening methods: personal references, employment references, address check, criminal background check, child abuse registry, driving record check, credit check, and drug testing.

5. Make sure the agency will provide you with copies of references and all available information concerning the employee's background.

6. Find out what special fees your family will be responsible for paying and what fees the caregiver must pay. For example, if the nanny hasn't received training in CPR or first aid, or if the nanny needs to recertify, who will pay for this? Who will pay for a physical or a drug screen for the nanny if one is requested?

7. Check with your local Better Business Bureau or the chamber of commerce to see if the agency is a member in good standing.

8. If an agency is a baby-sitting agency, then most likely it offers occasional sitters, and the company may be bonded to cover any

damages to the client. Be sure to check on
this.

9. Ask if the agency has any contract or
   agreement with their nannies that affects the
   relationship between the caregiver and the
   family. You will want to know if the agency
   has issued any binding contracts that will
   commit you to pay employee severance pay,
   insurance, or other costs you may not be
   aware of. Be sure that you know about all
   responsibilities placed on you or your employee by any contract between the agency
   and the employee.

10. Find out if the agency offers a payroll pro-
    gram or can refer you to someone who does.

11. If you decide to use an agency, prepare a
    written job description in advance for the
    kind of employee you need and show it to
    the agency. Include the salary you can af-
    ford to pay. (See Chapters 2 and 3 for
    examples.)

Children with Special Needs

Any child who has a physical disability or requires medical supervision is considered to have special needs. Once a child has been diagnosed as needing specialized short- or long-term care, the next step is to find the right caregiver. This chapter is dedicated to all families who are coping with finding care for children with special needs, and is designed to ease some of the difficulties your family will face when looking for child care.

Since special training is usually required, the cost of hiring qualified help for children with special needs is often higher than for regular child care, whether you hire a nanny or find a day care center that will take your child. These children do need more attention and care, so it's only logical for a care giver to expect to be paid more for the job. The salary will depend on the level of training the nanny has had and the amount of experience needed to provide care for your child. Salaries start at no less than $6 to $7 an hour and may run as high as $15 an hour if the nanny is medically trained or a certified nurse's assistant. You can call a home health aide agency or place an ad in the newspaper to find these applicants.

Finding Qualified In-home Caregivers

If your child has an emotional disorder or a physical disability that requires bed rest or special medication, in-home care is probably best for you. However, you will need to make sure that you hire someone who has the proper training to care for your child. A certified nursing assistant can handle most medication and doctor's orders, and won't cost as much as a nurse. You might also consider looking for a retired nurse who can use some extra income, or someone who has worked in a nursing home and might find it less stressful to work for a family. You can find these home care workers through home health agencies, or by placing an ad at nursing schools or in local newspapers as discussed in Chapter 4. Salaries usually range from $7 to $15 hourly, depending upon the applicant's experience and education. Finally, nannies usually don't mind taking classes or training deemed necessary to care for a child with special needs if the parent will pay for it. Just make sure that when all is said and done, the caregiver you hire is qualified to care for all of your child's needs and can handle any emergency that may arise. Don't forget that any individual offering in-home care needs, at the very least, basic training in first aid.

Day Care

It may take a bit of a search to find a day care center with staff members who are trained to care for children with special needs. You can start by looking in the yellow pages, or call your local family and human services center or YMCA for referrals. Happily, more centers today offer care for children with special needs than did so a decade ago.

When interviewing prospective caregivers, it's important to represent your child's needs as honestly and realistically as possible. The more truthful you are, the longer the caregiver will stay if hired. Don't overlook the fact that your child's size and weight may affect your search for a suitable nanny or caregiver. While parents may view their child or young adult as a helpless dependent, the child may actually require a caregiver who is much bigger or more physically fit than most nannies.

When interviewing in-home help or day care staff, don't forget to take your child's temperament into account, especially if the child is sensitive or emotionally disturbed. If possible, have the child meet the prospective caregiver.

How Do I Keep My Caregiver When I've Found the Right One?

The main complaint I hear from caregivers for special needs children is that while families understandably feel the need to take care of everything for the child, they often underestimate what a child can learn to do independently, and so make it more difficult for anyone else to care for the child on a regular basis. For example, if a nanny or therapist teaches a child how to help care for himself or herself, parents must make the effort to practice the new skills with their child, rather than decreasing the child's chances for independence by reverting to old habits because they are more convenient or save time.

The more self-sufficient a child is, the better. Moreover, nannies and other caregivers will be more likely to take a job where a child with special needs has some ability and initiative to help himself or herself, especially as the child grows older.

Here are some useful resources on caring for children with special needs:

ERIC Clearinghouse on Disabilities and Gifted
  Education
Council for Exceptional Children
1920 Association Drive
Reston, VA 22091–1589
Fax 707–264–9494

National Center for Learning Disabilities
99 Park Avenue
New York, NY 10016
212–545–7510

National Down's Syndrome Society
666 Broadway, Suite 810
New York, NY 10012
800–221–4602

National Easter Seals Society
70 East Lake Street
Chicago, IL 60601
312–726–6200

National Information Center for Children and
  Youth with Handicaps
P.O. Box 1492
Washington, DC 20013
Local Voice 703–893–6061; 703–893–8614
Toll Free 800–999–5599

United Cerebral Palsy
1522 K Street, N.W., No. 1112
Washington, DC 20005
800–872–5827

12

When You Can't Afford a Nanny

If you consider all your options and then decide that a day care center is all you can afford or is the best choice for your child, this chapter offers an overview of some of the most important things to consider in choosing a day care facility for your child.

In general:

- Look around to see if the facility is cheerful, clean and attractive, since your child will be there most of the day. Is there enough light and ventilation? Are the toys safe and clean?

- Look at the quality of the day care center's construction and equipment. Is everything safe and well-maintained?

- Review the safety regulations. Check to see if they fall within guidelines of the state where you live. (To check state laws on day care centers, contact the local office of the child welfare department.)

- Check all fire and other safety precautions at the day care center. Do they have fire extinguishers and smoke detectors? Are medicines and household products locked away?

As you tour the day care center or the family day care, consider the following questions:

1. Are the children happy?
2. What is the ratio of teachers to children at the center?
3. Is the teacher or provider listening to the children when they talk to her? Does she seem to enjoy the children?
4. Are the children handled gently and treated with individual care?
5. Are the children encouraged to express themselves?
6. Are activities varied and age-appropriate?
7. Is there time for children to work as a group?
8. Is the schedule of the day structured for the children's benefit?
9. What discipline is used at the facility?
10. What nutritional value do the daily meals provide for the children's dietary needs?
11. Are there restrictions on who is accepted at the day care facility, such as handicapped children or children on medication for health reasons?

12. Are the teachers certified in CPR? (In some states the law dictates that all workers must be certified in case of accidents in which a child stops breathing.)

13. Does the center have any equipment for medical emergencies? Find out what hospital the center uses in case of accidents or medical problems.

14. If the facility has a pool, is there adequate protection for the children around the pool area?

15. Does the staff mind if parents drop in during the day to visit and check on their child? Are parents encouraged to meet with the caregiver regularly?

16. Is any fee charged if parents are late picking up their child?

17. Is there a lot of staff turnover? (This could signal some problem with the center's operations. I hear stories from day care workers all the time about day care centers that are being run poorly by their owners.)

Day care centers should provide stimulation for children and encourage them to play together. Activities should allow the children to experiment with new materials and try new experiences: the toys at the center should challenge a child's learning skills; time should be set aside each day for outside play; opportunities should exist for trips away from the center for exposure to new people and situations. Such activities help children develop social skills and discover where they stand in the world around them.

If the children at a center you visit don't seem

happy, find out why. Make sure that the values in the center's program are compatible with yours and that the center will enhance your child's life and promote social interaction with other children. There's no getting around the fact that children don't like being left somewhere by their parents. So it's best to try to ensure that they will have fun and learn at the same time. Remember that the care you give your children when they are very young will affect their eventual attitudes toward school. You want your children to look forward to going to school, not to dislike it because of a past bad experience at a day care facility. Always check with the state authorities where you live to familiarize yourself with any laws concerning day care. Make sure the day care center you are interested in abides by all the state laws for the safety of your child or children.

Here are some requirements for day care centers that may be applicable in your state.

1. Operators of day care facilities must take an approved three-hour introductory course in child care.

2. Child care personnel in day care facilities are subject to applicable screening provisions determined by the state.

3. Day care facilities must annually register with the state their name and address, the name of their operator, the number of children to whom they provide care, and their emergency equipment. (Family day care facilities may be automatically licensed by the state if they are currently licensed by one of its counties.)

4. Basic information on day care centers is included in a directory published annually by
the state department of licensing.

5. The state department of licensing must prepare a brochure on family day care that
includes:

   a. A brief description of the requirements
   for day care registration, including training, fingerprinting, and screening.

   b. A listing of counties that require licenses
   for day care facilities and information
   concerning the licensing.

   c. Information about how to obtain a statement about compliance with state law
   and local requirements by day care
   facilities.

   d. Reports of suspected and actual abuses
   by day care centers and any other information relating to competent child care
   that the department or local licensing
   agencies deem helpful to the public.

6. The licensing department may also prepare
an annual evaluation of the registration and
licensure system for day care facilities that
includes, at a minimum, the following:

   a. The number of day care centers
   registered.

   b. The number of children cared for by day
   care centers.

   c. The number of complaints concerning
   day care centers.

   d. The training activities used by the day

care centers, according to local training requirements.

7. To inform the public of the state requirements for registration of family day care homes and other requirements for such homes to operate legally, the state may institute a media campaign via flyers, television, radio, or newspaper advertisements.

Licensing standards for child care facilities generally apply to the following areas:

1. Personnel—Standards for child care personnel, whether employees or volunteers, include minimum age requirements of employees, minimum staff training requirements for identification and reporting of child abuse and neglect, periodic health examinations, minimum levels of training in first aid, and ratios of personnel to children.

2. Physical facilities—Standards include minimums for building condition, indoor play space, outdoor play space, napping space, bathroom facilities, food preparation facilities, outdoor and indoor equipment.

3. Sanitation and safety—Standards exist for sanitary and safety conditions, first aid treatment, and emergency procedures.

4. Nutritional practices—Standards are established for the provision of meals or snacks of sufficient quality and quantity to assure that the nutritional needs of children are met.

5. Admissions and record keeping—Requirements govern preadmission and periodic

health examinations, immunizations, and the maintenance of emergency information and health records for all children. Any child may be exempted from medical or physical examination, or medical or surgical treatment, upon written request of the child's parent or guardian who objects to the examination or treatment. However, no laws, rules, and regulations relating to contagious or communicable diseases and sanitary matters shall be violated.

6. Transportation safety—Requirements are set for child restraints or seatbelts in vehicles used by child care facilities to transport children, for annual inspections of the vehicles, for limitations on facilities to transport children, for annual inspections of the vehicles, and for limitations on the number of children in the vehicles.

7. Access—Standards provide for reasonable access to the child care facility by the custodial parent or guardian during the time the child is in care.

8. Child discipline—Standards for child discipline practices ensure that age-appropriate, constructive disciplinary practices are used for children in care. Such standards include at least the following minimum requirements:

   a. Children shall not be subject to discipline that is severe, humiliating, or frightening.

   b. Discipline shall not be associated with food, rest, or toileting.

   c. Spanking or any other form of physical punishment is prohibited.

9. Plan of activities—Standards ensure that each
   child care facility implements a written plan
   for daily provision of varied activities and ac-
   tive and quiet play opportunities appropriate
   to the age of the children.

Appendix A

NANNY TRAINING SCHOOLS IN THE UNITED STATES

The Complete Nanny Guide can't guarantee that the information is accurate or that the schools, agencies, and services listed provide quality services or training. Please check with the schools, agencies, and services to verify the information listed.

Arkansas

Quapaw Technical
  Institute
200 Mid-American
  Boulevard
Hot Springs, AR 71913
501–767–9314

California

American Nanny College
P.O. Box 790
Claremont, CA 95825
800–462–7711;
714–624–7711

American Nanny College
4650 Arrow Highway,
  Suite A-10
Montclair, CA 91763
909–624–7711

Colorado

Colorado Nanny
  Academy
17800 County Road 20
Fort Morgan, CO 80701
303–867–6608

Morgan Community
  College
17800 County Road 20
Fort Morgan, CO 80701
303–867–3081

Illinois

Care-4-Kids, Inc.
1207 Glencoe Avenue
Highland Park, IL
  60035–4007
708–433–4737

Carl Sandburg College
2232 South Lake Storey
Galesburg, IL 61401
309–433–4738

Kentucky

Nannies of Kentucky
4300 West Highway 146
Crestwood, KY 40014
502–222–7690

Massachusetts

Caregivers Training
  School
155 Chestnut Street
West Springfield, MA
  01103
413–737–2525

Michigan

Delta College
University Center, MI
  48710
517–686–9543

Nannies of America
4190 Telegraph, Suite
  3300
Bloomfield Hills, MI
  48302
313–540–4960

Minnesota

Red Wing Technical
  College
5354 Moundsview Drive
Red Wing, MN 55066
800–657–4849

Montana

Montana Nannies, Inc.
101 Eleventh Avenue
    South
Shelby, MT 59474
406–434–2502

Nebraska

Central Community
    College
East Highway 6
Hastings, NE 68901
402–463–9811

Central Community
    College
512 West 11th Street
Kearney, NE 68847
308–237–2379

Central Community
    College
613 North Washington
    Street
Lexington, NE 68850
308–324–5936

Muffy Vrana &
    Company
3260 Van Dorn
Lincoln, NE 68502
402–488–0316

Southeast Community
    College
Lincoln, NE 68520
402–437–2455

Nevada

Nanny's & Granny's
6440 West Coley
Las Vegas, NV 89102
702–364–5901

Nanny's & Granny's
South Highland Drive
Las Vegas, NV 89103
702–368–7741

Nanny's & Granny's
3790 Redwood Street
Las Vegas, NV 89103
702–362–9255

New Jersey

Nanny's & Granny's
Neighborhood Nannies
    205
Haddonfield, NJ 08033
609–795–5833

New Mexico

NMSU Dona Ana Branch
  Community College
Box 30001, Department 3
  D.A.
Las Cruces, NM 88003
505–527–7515

University of New Mex-
  ico, Los Alamos
400 University Drive
Los Alamos, NM 87544
505–622–5919

New York

Sullivan County Com-
  munity College
Early Childhood
  Programs
Box 4002
Loch Sheldrake, NY
  12759
914–434–5750

Ohio

English Nanny & Gov-
  erness School
30 South Franklin
Chagrin Falls, OH 44022
216–247–0600
Fax: 800–733–1984

Oklahoma

Demarge College
3608 N.W. 58th Street
Oklahoma City, OK
  73112
405–947–1534

Metro Tech Vocational
  Technical
District Number 22
3901 North Martin Lu-
  ther Boulevard
Oklahoma City, OK
  73111
405–424–8324

Murray State College
Route 1, Box 84
Tishominga, OK 73460
405–371–2371

Northeastern Oklahoma
  A&M College
Box 3894
Miami, OK 74354
918–542–8441

Pennsylvania

Community College of
  Allegheny County
North Campus, 8701
  Perry Highway
Pittsburgh, PA 15237
412–369–3624

Vermont

The Connection School
  for Nannies
207–232 Skitchwaug
  Trail
Springfield, VT 05156
802–885–3556

Virginia

New World Nannies,
  Inc.
8706 Melwood Lane
Richmond, VA 23229
804–282–6128

Wisconsin

Moraine Park Technical
  College
235 North National
  Avenue
Fond Du Lac, WI 54936
800–472–4554;
414–922–8611

Moraine Park Technical
  College
700 Gould Street
Beaver Dam, WI 53916
414–887–1101

Moraine Park Technical
  College
742 Greentree Mall
Berlin, WI 54923
414–361–3601

Appendix B1

APPLICATION FOR NANNY/HELPMATE

Name (First/Middle/Last) _____

Address _____

_____

City/State/Zip Code _____

Home/Work Phone Number _____

Social Security Number _____

Date of Birth _____

If married, spouse's name (First/Middle/Last) _____

_____

Spouse's Work Phone Number _____

Spouse's Social Security Number _____

How many dependents do you have? _____

Your children's ages are: _____

If your children were sick, would you have someone to help care for them or would you have to
miss work? _____

Application for Nanny/Helpmate (cont'd)

Elementary Grade Finished _____

High School Grade Finished _____

College or Technical School Training _____
_____

List any other training. _____
_____

Have you ever been bonded or licensed? _____

If so, please give the organization's name, address, and phone number. _____
_____
_____

Have you received CPR or first aid training? _____

Would you be willing to take CPR training if asked to for the job? _____

Starting with most recent job, list your past employers, positions, and salaries—including names, addresses, and phone numbers—for the past three years. _____
_____
_____
_____
_____
_____
_____

Application for Nanny/Helpmate (cont'd)

List your previous address(es) for the past three years.

_____

_____

_____

_____

_____

How long have you lived in this state? _____

List three personal references, including addresses
and phone numbers.

1. _____

_____

2. _____

_____

3. _____

_____

Are you an American citizen? _____

If not, do you have a green card or visa to work in
this country? _____

Have you ever been in the military? _____

Do you have a driver's license? _____

If so, please specify number, state, and expiration
date. _____

Has your license ever been revoked? _____

Have you ever been charged with or convicted of
driving under the influence of alcohol? _____

Application for Nanny/Helpmate (cont'd)

How far do you live from the job? _____

Do you have your own transportation? _____

Do you have a religious preference that may require time away from the job? If so, please specify. ____

_____

Do you have any health problem(s) that would interfere with your job. Please explain.

_____

_____

_____

Are you currently taking any medication? Please explain. _____

_____

_____

Have you suffered from any kind of substance abuse? _____

Would you submit to a drug screen? _____

When was your last physical exam? _____

Have you ever been charged with or convicted of any kind of child abuse? _____

Have you ever been charged with or convicted of a crime? _____

Has anyone you live with been charged with or convicted of a crime? _____

Application for Nanny/Helpmate (cont'd)

Do you smoke? _____

Do you prefer a nonsmoking family? _____

Are you allergic to or afraid of pets or animals? ____

Who should be contacted in case of emergency
(please include name, address, and day and eve-
ning phone numbers): _____

_____

_____

_____

Work hours preferred: _____

Preferred salary: _____

Are you willing to stay overnight occasionally? ____

Are you available on weekends? _____

Will you work more than forty hours a week if
necessary? _____

If so, list how many hours overtime you will be willing to work. _____

Would you agree to travel with the family or relocate
if asked to? _____

All of the information on this application is true to
the best of my knowledge. I understand that if any
criminal conduct is discovered, I can be discharged
from my job immediately.

Signed: _____

Date: _____

Appendix B2

CHECKLIST FOR SCREENING NANNY/HELPMATE

Name _____

Address _____

_____

_____

_____

Phone Number _____

Date _____

Time _____

COMMENTS

1. On time _____
2. Experience _____

_____

_____

Checklist for Screening
Nanny/Helpmate (cont'd)

_____

_____

_____

3. Duration of last job _____

4. Work attitude _____

5. Work goals _____

_____

_____

_____

_____

_____

6. Character _____

7. Appearance _____

_____

8. Strong points _____

_____

_____

_____

_____

9. Weak points _____

_____

Checklist for Screening
Nanny/Helpmate (cont'd)

_____

_____

_____

10. Transportation _____

11. Hours wanted _____

12. Salary expected _____

Notes

_____

_____

_____

_____

_____

_____

_____

_____

_____

_____

_____

_____

_____

_____

Appendix C1

EMPLOYMENT AND CHARACTER REFERENCE RELEASE FORM

Beginning with most recent job, list your past employers below, along with their names and phone numbers.

Name of employer or family _____

_____

Address _____

_____

_____

City/State/Zip Code _____

Phone Number _____

Number of children in your care and ages _____

_____

_____

Reasons for leaving _____

_____

_____

_____

Salary paid _____

Employment and Character Reference
Release Form (cont'd)

Name of employer or family _____

Address _____

_____

City/State/Zip Code _____
Phone Number _____
Number of children in your care and ages _____

_____

_____

Reasons for leaving _____

_____

_____

_____

Salary paid _____

Name of employer or family _____

Address _____

_____

City/State/Zip Code _____
Phone Number _____
Number of children in your care and ages _____

_____

_____

Reasons for leaving _____

_____

_____

_____

Salary paid _____

Employment and Character Reference
Release Form (cont'd)

CHARACTER REFERENCES
Please list the names, addresses, and phone numbers of three people you have known for one year or more, who are not family members.

1. Name _____
Address _____
City/State/Zip Code _____
Phone Number_____Known from_____to _____

2. Name _____
Address _____
City/State/Zip Code _____
Phone Number_____Known from_____to _____

3. Name _____
Address _____
City/State/Zip Code _____
Phone Number_____Known from_____to _____

The facts I have listed are true. By my signature I give permission for any information regarding my personal, employment, or credit history to be released to the person requesting such information. I understand that if any of the preceding information is false, I can lose my job immediately.

Signature _____
Date _____

Appendix C2

EMPLOYEE PERFORMANCE REQUEST FORM

[Applicant's name] has applied for work in our home and has listed you as an employer from [date] to [date]. We would appreciate your answering the following questions pertaining to [applicant's name] work performance. Thank you.

Employer's Name _____

Address _____

_____

_____

City/State/Zip Code _____

Applicant's Salary _____

Reasons for Leaving _____

_____

_____

_____

_____

Employee Performance Request Form (cont'd)

Would you hire this person again to work for your family? _____

_____

_____

_____

_____

Please check:

Work quality was Good _____ Fair _____ Excellent _____

Job attitude was   Good _____ Fair _____ Excellent _____

Employee was on time Always _____ Sometimes _____ Never _____

If there were problems with the employee's work, please state the reasons and circumstances. _____

_____

_____

_____

_____

List any additional information that could help us in our decision.

_____

_____

_____

_____

_____

[Prospective Employer's Signature] _____

Date _____

Appendix C3

CRIMINAL BACKGROUND
RELEASE FORM

[Employer's Name and Address]

_____

_____

_____

[Employer] is requesting a criminal background release on the individual named below, who is to be employed for the care of children.

Date _____

Name _____

Date of Birth _____

Race _____

Social Security Number _____

Criminal Background Release Form (cont'd)

Alias names used (including all maiden or married names used by applicant)

_____

_____

_____

_____

I understand and agree to any criminal background check for the benefit of the individual named above.

I ____[applicant]____ give permission and agree by my signature to the release of any and all such information to __[employer]__ .

Applicant Signature _____ Date _____

Employer Signature _____ Date _____

Appendix C4

CRIMINAL BACKGROUND INFORMATION SOURCES IN THE UNITED STATES

**Alabama State Human
 Services**
205–298–7882

Alabama State Patrol
205–865–3451

Alaska State Troopers
907–766–2552;
907–438–2019

**Arizona State
 Government**
602–921–4400

**Arizona Law
 Enforcement**
602–223–2515

**Arkansas Highway
 Patrol**
501–247–1483

California State Police
916–445–1150

Colorado State Highway
303–824–5010

Connecticut State Police
203–347–4333;
203–623–3634

**Delaware State Police
 Troop**
302–577–3008;
302–577–3051

Florida Department of Law Enforcement
904–488–5081

Georgia Criminal Information Department
404–244–2601

Georgia State Human Resource
404–358–2657

Hawaii State Police
808–732–0727

Illinois Criminal Justice Department
312–793–8550

Indiana State Police
219–636–2262

Iowa State Patrol
319–385–8715

Kansas State Highway Department
316–723–2503

Kentucky State Police
502–826–3312

Louisiana Criminal Justice Department
504–922–6095

Louisiana State Police
504–295–8500

Maine State Police
207–793–4500

Maryland State Police
410–486–3101

Massachusetts Department of Public Safety
617–566–4500

Michigan State Police
517–362–3434

Michigan State Transportation Department
616–979–1170

Minnesota Department of Public Safety
612–642–0670

Mississippi State Government
601–939–8640

Missouri Highway Patrol
314–751–3313

Montana State Highway Patrol
406–365–5238

Nebraska State Patrol
402–475–4545

Nevada Highway Patrol
702–486–4100

**New Hampshire Safety
Department**
603–358–3333

**New Hampshire State
Police**
603–846–5517

**New Jersey Criminal
Justice Department**
609–984–6500

**New Jersey State
Department**
609–292–2121

**New Mexico State
Government**
505–461–1206

**New York Department
of Justice**
518–457–6113

**North Carolina State
Government**
919–274–1681

**North Carolina State
Patrol**
919–747–2420

**North Dakota Highway
Patrol**
701–774–4360

**North Dakota Human
Service**
701–255–3090

Ohio State Police
419–826–5871;
419–599–0991

**Oklahoma State High-
way Patrol**
918–968–3000;
405–258–0494

**Oregon State Depart-
ment of Police Public
Service**
503–378–3720

**Pennsylvania State
Patrol**
717–783–5588

**Rhode Island Sheriff's
Office**
401–841–8300

Rhode Island State
Police
401–846–8200

South Carolina State
Highway Patrol
803–874–4141;
803–882–5679

South Dakota State
Patrol
605–339–6601

Tennessee Sheriff's
Office
615–862–8123

Texas Criminal Justice
Department
512–465–2151;
512–463–9988;
512–463–0345

Utah State Government
801–752–2511

Utah State Highway
Patrol
801–654–2073

Utah State Human
Service
801–586–3841

Vermont State Police,
Beheld
802–234–9933

Vermont State Police,
Enosburg
802–933–5555

Virginia State Police
804–674–2000

Washington, D.C. Crimi-
nal Justice
202–324–5278

West Virginia State
Police
304–843–4100;
304–824–5798

Wisconsin State Patrol
608–269–2500;
715–386–3248

Wyoming State
Government
307–469–2234

Wyoming State Patrol
307–754–3666

Appendix D1

NAP NOTES FOR NANNY AND CHILD

This chart is designed for use as a record and reminder
of daily activities.

Week of _____ to _____

Daily Chart	MONDAY	TUESDAY	WEDNESDAY
Breakfast			
Play time			
Lunch Nap time			
Accidents Achievements			
Vitamins Medicines			
Sickness			
Change of clothes Baths			
Activities (walks, stories, videos, games)			
Comments on events Time out, etc.			
Child's laundry			
Vacuum child's room			
Miscellaneous notes by parents			

THURSDAY	FRIDAY	SATURDAY	SUNDAY

Appendix D2

PARENT AND NANNY AGREEMENT (#1)

1. This agreement covers the time period from _____ to _____.

2. Termination of agreement
a. If the employee is terminated for just cause, the employer is not bound to this agreement; however, one week's severance pay will be given, after the employee has worked _____ months.
b. If the employee voluntarily decides to leave the position, the employee will provide the employer with at least _____ weeks' notice.
c. If the employer has incurred any outstanding bills on the behalf of the employee, the sum total may be deducted from the employee's pay at the time of the employee's termination.

3. This agreement and any part thereof may be amended at any time with the mutual agreement and signature of all parties.

Parent and Nanny Agreement (cont'd)

4. Review of agreement, performance, and salary is mutually agreed to be set for the following dates [Quarterly, etc.]:

Date _____ Date _____ Date _____

5. This full-time child care position includes but is not limited to the following responsibilities:

    a. To provide child care up to _____ hours per day, for _____ days per week.

    b. To provide light housekeeping, which means any child care-related duties (i.e., preparing food, cleaning up after meals, child's laundry).

    c. To comply with parent's discipline and child rearing preferences.

    d. To use creative skills in planning activities that promote the physical, emotional, intellectual, and social development of the child, as approved by the parent or guardian.

    e. To promote feelings of security and warmth by planning daily cuddle/reading/talk time with each child.

    f. To maintain a cheerful and helpful attitude while on duty.

    g. To write daily log sheets of events and to confer with parents about special problems, child's newly learned skills, etc., so as to promote good communication with parents concerning child's daytime life.

    h. To provide reasonable flexibility in the time of emergency or unexpected schedule changes.

    i. To read/review any pertinent literature provided by parents to promote broader knowledge of child rearing philosophy, education, or child psychology.

Parent and Nanny Agreement (cont'd)

6. **Additional responsibilities**
   a. Child's bedroom and playroom to be kept tidy; crib sheets to be changed once a week.
   b. Child's bedroom and playroom to be vacuumed once a week.
   c. Diaper pail to be emptied into garage trashcans daily.
   d. Formula bottles to be prepared as needed.
   e. Child to be provided with a minimum of two hours of fresh air daily, weather permitting.
   f. Child to be bathed as needed or if requested by parent.
   g. Dishwasher to be loaded, unloaded, or run as needed.
   h. Pets to be fed daily.
   i. Parent's laundry to be done upon request.
   j. Parent's dinner to be defrosted or prepared upon request.

7. **Transporting child**
Child is not to be transported anywhere without permission of parents.

8. **Work schedule**
Monday through Friday _____ A.M. to _____ P.M. or up to _____ hours per day, with the total not to exceed 50 hours per week.

9. **Compensation**
   a. Employers agree to pay the employee a base salary of $ _____ per week from [date] until [date] and then to pay $ _____ per week beginning [date].

Parent and Nanny Agreement (cont'd)

b. Salary is to be paid every week on Friday for the period of Monday through Friday of the previous week.

c. Overtime compensation is to be paid at a rate of $ _____ per hour or at 1½ times the hourly rate of current salary.

10. Taxes

a. The employer will withhold the appropriate taxes and social security from the employee's salary.

b. If an independent contractor, the employee is responsible to report all earned income and to pay all appropriate taxes. Employee can be given a Form 1099.

11. Vacation

Employers agree to allow the employee one week of vacation to be taken after _____ months of employment.

Employer _____ **Date** _____
Employer _____ **Date** _____
Employee _____ **Date** _____

PARENT AND NANNY AGREEMENT (#2)

The following is an example of an independent contract that can be used if the nanny or housekeeper is considered self-employed.

Independent Contracting Agreement

_____[Employer]_____, referred to as contracting party, and _____[Employee]_____, referred to as independent contractor, agree:

Independent contractor shall perform the following services for contracting party: _____ at the following rate of remuneration: _____. This agreement shall begin on _____ and shall terminate on _____ unless terminated in the following circumstance. Contracting party may terminate this contract at any time on fourteen days' notice to independent contractor for unsatisfactory performance.

This is an agreement for independent contracting services. The contracting party provides no benefits such as unemployment insurance, health insurance, or worker's compensation insurance to independent contractor. Independent contractor is responsible for payment of all federal, state, and local taxes.

Contracting party _____ Date _____
Independent contractor _____ Date _____

Appendix E1

Form SS-4
(Rev. December 1993)
Department of the Treasury
Internal Revenue Service

Application for Employer Identification Number

(For use by employers, corporations, partnerships, trusts, estates, churches, government agencies, certain individuals, and others. See instructions.)

EIN

OMB No. 1545-0003
Expires 12-31-96

Please type or print clearly.

1 Name of applicant (Legal name) (See instructions.)

2 Trade name of business, if different from name in line 1

3 Executor, trustee, "care of" name

4a Mailing address (street address) (room, apt., or suite no.)

5a Business address, if different from address in lines 4a and 4b

4b City, state, and ZIP code

5b City, state, and ZIP code

6 County and state where principal business is located

7 Name of principal officer, general partner, grantor, owner, or trustor—SSN required (See instructions.) ▶

8a Type of entity (Check only one box.) (See instructions.)
☐ Sole Proprietor (SSN) _____
☐ REMIC   ☐ Personal service corp.
☐ State/local government ☐ National guard
☐ Other nonprofit organization (specify) _____
☐ Other (specify) ▶

☐ Estate (SSN of decedent) _____
☐ Plan administrator-SSN _____
☐ Other corporation (specify) _____
☐ Federal government/military ☐ Church or church controlled organization
_____ (enter GEN if applicable) _____

☐ Trust
☐ Partnership
☐ Farmers' cooperative

8b If a corporation, name the state or foreign country (if applicable) where incorporated ▶

State

Foreign country

9 Reason for applying (Check only one box.)
☐ Started new business (specify) ▶ _____
☐ Hired employees
☐ Created a pension plan (specify type) ▶ _____
☐ Banking purpose (specify) ▶

☐ Changed type of organization (specify) ▶ _____
☐ Purchased going business
☐ Created a trust (specify) ▶ _____
☐ Other (specify) ▶

10 Date business started or acquired (Mo., day, year) (See instructions.)

11 Enter closing month of accounting year. (See instructions.)

12 First date wages or annuities were paid or will be paid (Mo., day, year). **Note:** *If applicant is a withholding agent, enter date income will first be paid to nonresident alien. (Mo., day, year)* . . . . ▶

13 Enter highest number of employees expected in the next 12 months. **Note:** *If the applicant does not expect to have any employees during the period, enter "0."* . . . . ▶

Nonagricultural	Agricultural	Household

14 Principal activity (See instructions.) ▶

15 Is the principal business activity manufacturing? . . . . ☐ Yes ☐ No
If "Yes," principal product and raw material used ▶

16 To whom are most of the products or services sold? Please check the appropriate box.   ☐ Business (wholesale)
☐ Public (retail)   ☐ Other (specify) ▶   ☐ N/A

17a Has the applicant ever applied for an identification number for this or any other business? . . . . ☐ Yes ☐ No
Note: *If "Yes," please complete lines 17b and 17c.*

17b If you checked the "Yes" box in line 17a, give applicant's legal name and trade name, if different than name shown on prior application.

Legal name ▶   Trade name ▶

17c Enter approximate date, city, and state where the application was filed and the previous employer identification number if known.
Approximate date when filed (Mo., day, year) | City and state where filed | Previous EIN

Under penalties of perjury, I declare that I have examined this application, and to the best of my knowledge and belief, it is true, correct, and complete.

Business telephone number (include area code)

Name and title (Please type or print clearly.) ▶

Signature ▶   Date ▶

Note: *Do not write below this line.   For official use only.*

Please leave blank ▶	Geo.	Ind.	Class	Size	Reason for applying

For Paperwork Reduction Act Notice, see attached instructions.   Cat. No. 16055N   Form **SS-4** (Rev. 12-93)

Appendix E2

a Control number	22222	Void ☐	For Official Use Only ▶ OMB No. 1545-0008		
b Employer's identification number				1 Wages, tips, other compensation	2 Federal income tax withheld
c Employer's name, address, and ZIP code				3 Social security wages	4 Social security tax withheld
				5 Medicare wages and tips	6 Medicare tax withheld
				7 Social security tips	8 Allocated tips
d Employee's social security number				9 Advance EIC payment	10 Dependent care benefits
e Employee's name (first, middle initial, last)				11 Nonqualified plans	12 Benefits included in box 1
				13 See Instrs. for box 13	14 Other
				15 Statutory employee ☐ Deceased ☐ Pension plan ☐ Legal rep. ☐ 942 emp. ☐ Subtotal ☐ Deferred compensation ☐	
f Employee's address and ZIP code					
16 State Employer's state I.D. No.	17 State wages, tips, etc.	18 State income tax	19 Locality name	20 Local wages, tips, etc.	21 Local income tax

Cat. No. 10134D   Department of the Treasury—Internal Revenue Service

Form **W-2** Wage and Tax Statement **1994**   For Paperwork Reduction Act Notice, see separate instructions.

Copy A For Social Security Administration

Do NOT Cut or Separate Forms on This Page

a Control number	22222	Void ☐	For Official Use Only ▶ OMB No. 1545-0008		
b Employer's identification number				1 Wages, tips, other compensation	2 Federal income tax withheld
c Employer's name, address, and ZIP code				3 Social security wages	4 Social security tax withheld
				5 Medicare wages and tips	6 Medicare tax withheld
				7 Social security tips	8 Allocated tips
d Employee's social security number				9 Advance EIC payment	10 Dependent care benefits
e Employee's name (first, middle initial, last)				11 Nonqualified plans	12 Benefits included in box 1
				13 See Instrs. for box 13	14 Other
				15 Statutory employee ☐ Deceased ☐ Pension plan ☐ Legal rep. ☐ 942 emp. ☐ Subtotal ☐ Deferred compensation ☐	
f Employee's address and ZIP code					
16 State Employer's state I.D. No.	17 State wages, tips, etc.	18 State income tax	19 Locality name	20 Local wages, tips, etc.	21 Local income tax

Cat. No. 10134D   Department of the Treasury—Internal Revenue Service

Form **W-2** Wage and Tax Statement **1994**   For Paperwork Reduction Act Notice, see separate instructions.

Copy A For Social Security Administration

Appendix E3

Form W-4 (1995)

Want More Money In Your Paycheck? If you expect to be able to take the earned income credit for 1995 and a child lives with you, you may be able to have part of the credit added to your take-home pay. For details, get Form W-5 from your employer.

Purpose. Complete Form W-4 so that your employer can withhold the correct amount of Federal income tax from your pay.

Exemption From Withholding. Read line 7 of the certificate below to see if you can claim exempt status. If exempt, complete line 7; but do not complete lines 5 and 6. No Federal income tax will be withheld from your pay. Your exemption is good for 1 year only. It expires February 15, 1996.

Note: You cannot claim exemption from withholding if (1) your income exceeds $650 and includes unearned income (e.g., interest

and dividends) and (2) another person can claim you as a dependent on their tax return.

Basic Instructions. Employees who are not exempt should complete the Personal Allowances Worksheet. Additional worksheets are provided on page 2 for employees to adjust their withholding allowances based on itemized deductions, adjustments to income, or two-earner/two-job situations. Complete all worksheets that apply to your situation. The worksheets will help you figure the number of withholding allowances you are entitled to claim. However, you may claim fewer allowances than this.

Head of Household. Generally, you may claim head of household filing status on your tax return only if you are unmarried and pay more than 50% of the costs of keeping up a home for yourself and your dependent(s) or other qualifying individuals.

Nonwage Income. If you have a large amount of nonwage income, such as interest or dividends, you should consider making

estimated tax payments using Form 1040-ES. Otherwise, you may find that you owe additional tax at the end of the year.

Two Earners/Two Jobs. If you have a working spouse or more than one job, figure the total number of allowances you are entitled to claim on all jobs using worksheets from only one Form W-4. This total should be divided among all jobs. Your withholding will usually be most accurate when all allowances are claimed on the W-4 filed for the highest paying job and zero allowances are claimed for the others.

Check Your Withholding. After your W-4 takes effect, you can use Pub. 919, Is My Withholding Correct for 1995?, to see how the dollar amount you are having withheld compares to your estimated total annual tax. We recommend you get Pub. 919 especially if you used the Two Earner/Two Job Worksheet and your earnings exceed $150,000 (Single) or $200,000 (Married). Call 1-800-829-3676 to order Pub. 919. Check your telephone directory for the IRS assistance number for further help.

Personal Allowances Worksheet

A Enter "1" for **yourself** if no one else can claim you as a dependent . . . . **A** _____

B Enter "1" if:
- You are single and have only one job; or
- You are married, have only one job, and your spouse does not work; or
- Your wages from a second job or your spouse's wages (or the total of both) are $1,000 or less.

. . **B** _____

C Enter "1" for your **spouse**. But, you may choose to enter -0- if you are married and have either a working spouse or more than one job (this may help you avoid having too little tax withheld) . . . . **C** _____

D Enter number of **dependents** (other than your spouse or yourself) you will claim on your tax return . . . . . **D** _____

E Enter "1" if you will file as **head of household** on your tax return (see conditions under **Head of Household** above) . **E** _____

F Enter "1" if you have at least $1,500 of **child or dependent care expenses** for which you plan to claim a credit . **F** _____

G Add lines A through F and enter total here. Note:-This amount may be different from the number of exemptions you claim on your return ▶ **G** _____

For accuracy, do all worksheets that apply.
- If you plan to **itemize or claim adjustments to income** and want to reduce your withholding, see the Deductions and Adjustments Worksheet on page 2.
- If you are **single** and have **more than one job** and your combined earnings from all jobs exceed $30,000 OR if you are **married** and have a **working spouse or more than one job**, and the combined earnings from all jobs exceed $50,000, see the Two-Earner/Two-Job Worksheet on page 2 if you want to avoid having too little tax withheld.
- If **neither** of the above situations applies, **stop here** and enter the number from line G on line 5 of Form W-4 below.

·············· **Cut here and give the certificate to your employer. Keep the top portion for your records.** ··············

Form **W-4**
Department of the Treasury
Internal Revenue Service

Employee's Withholding Allowance Certificate

▶ **For Privacy Act and Paperwork Reduction Act Notice, see reverse.**

OMB No. 1545-0010

1995

1 Type or print your first name and middle initial	Last name	2 Your social security number

Home address (number and street or rural route)	3 ☐ Single ☐ Married ☐ Married, but withhold at higher Single rate. Note: If married, but legally separated, or spouse is a nonresident alien, check the Single box.
City or town, state, and ZIP code	4 If your last name differs from that on your social security card, check here and call 1-800-772-1213 for a new card . . . . . . ▶ ☐

5 Total number of allowances you are claiming (from line G above or from the worksheets on page 2 if they apply) . **5** _____

6 Additional amount, if any, you want withheld from each paycheck . . . . **6** $ _____

7 I claim exemption from withholding for 1995 and I certify that I meet **BOTH** of the following conditions for exemption:
- Last year I had a right to a refund of **ALL** Federal income tax withheld because I had **NO** tax liability; **AND**
- This year I expect a refund of **ALL** Federal income tax withheld because I expect to have **NO** tax liability.

If you meet both conditions, enter "EXEMPT" here . . . . ▶ **7** _____

Under penalties of perjury, I certify that I am entitled to the number of withholding allowances claimed on this certificate or entitled to claim exempt status.

Employee's signature ▶ _____ Date ▶ _____ , 19 ____

8 Employer's name and address (Employer: Complete 8 and 10 only if sending to the IRS)	9 Office code (optional)	10 Employer identification number

Cat. No. 10220Q

Form W-4 (cont'd)

Form W-4 (1995) | Page **2**

Deductions and Adjustments Worksheet

Note: *Use this worksheet only if you plan to itemize deductions or claim adjustments to income on your 1995 tax return.*

1   Enter an estimate of your 1995 itemized deductions. These include qualifying home mortgage interest, charitable contributions, state and local taxes (but not sales taxes), medical expenses in excess of 7.5% of your income, and miscellaneous deductions. (For 1995, you may have to reduce your itemized deductions if your income is over $114,700 ($57,350 if married filing separately). Get Pub. 919 for details.)   **1** $ _____

2   Enter: { $6,550 if married filing jointly or qualifying widow(er) / $5,750 if head of household / $3,900 if single / $3,275 if married filing separately }   **2** $ _____

3   **Subtract** line 2 from line 1. If line 2 is greater than line 1, enter -0-   **3** $ _____

4   Enter an estimate of your 1995 adjustments to income. These include alimony paid and deductible IRA contributions   **4** $ _____

5   **Add** lines 3 and 4 and enter the total   **5** $ _____

6   Enter an estimate of your 1995 nonwage income (such as dividends or interest)   **6** $ _____

7   **Subtract** line 6 from line 5. Enter the result, but not less than -0-   **7** $ _____

8   **Divide** the amount on line 7 by $2,500 and enter the result here. Drop any fraction   **8**   _____

9   Enter the number from Personal Allowances Worksheet, line G, on page 1   **9**   _____

10   **Add** lines 8 and 9 and enter the total here. If you plan to use the Two-Earner/Two-Job Worksheet, also enter this total on line 1 below. Otherwise, **stop here** and enter this total on Form W-4, line 5, on page 1   **10**   _____

Two-Earner/Two-Job Worksheet

Note: *Use this worksheet only if the instructions for line G on page 1 direct you here.*

1   Enter the number from line G on page 1 (or from line 10 above if you used the Deductions and Adjustments Worksheet)   **1**   _____

2   Find the number in Table 1 below that applies to the **LOWEST** paying job and enter it here   **2**   _____

3   If line 1 is **GREATER THAN OR EQUAL TO** line 2, subtract line 2 from line 1. Enter the result here (if zero, enter -0-) and on Form W-4, line 5, on page 1. **DO NOT** use the rest of this worksheet   **3**   _____

Note: *If line 1 is **LESS THAN** line 2, enter -0- on Form W-4, line 5, on page 1. Complete lines 4–9 to calculate the additional withholding amount necessary to avoid a year end tax bill.*

4   Enter the number from line 2 of this worksheet   **4**   _____

5   Enter the number from line 1 of this worksheet   **5**   _____

6   **Subtract** line 5 from line 4   **6**   _____

7   Find the amount in Table 2 below that applies to the **HIGHEST** paying job and enter it here   **7** $ _____

8   **Multiply** line 7 by line 6 and enter the result here. This is the additional annual withholding amount needed   **8** $ _____

9   Divide line 8 by the number of pay periods remaining in 1995. (For example, divide by 26 if you are paid every other week and you complete this form in December 1994.) Enter the result here and on Form W-4, line 6, page 1. This is the additional amount to be withheld from each paycheck   **9** $ _____

Table 1: Two-Earner/Two-Job Worksheet

Married Filing Jointly				All Others	
If wages from **LOWEST** paying job are—	Enter on line 2 above	If wages from **LOWEST** paying job are—	Enter on line 2 above	If wages from **LOWEST** paying job are—	Enter on line 2 above
0 - $3,000	0	39,001 - 50,000	9	0 - $4,000	0
3,001 - 6,000	1	50,001 - 55,000	10	4,001 - 10,000	1
6,001 - 11,000	2	55,001 - 60,000	11	10,001 - 14,000	2
11,001 - 16,000	3	60,001 - 70,000	12	14,001 - 19,000	3
16,001 - 21,000	4	70,001 - 80,000	13	19,001 - 23,000	4
21,001 - 27,000	5	80,001 - 90,000	14	23,001 - 45,000	5
27,001 - 31,000	6	90,001 and over	15	45,001 - 60,000	6
31,001 - 34,000	7			60,001 - 70,000	7
34,001 - 39,000	8			70,001 and over	8

Table 2: Two-Earner/Two-Job Worksheet

Married Filing Jointly		All Others	
If wages from **HIGHEST** paying job are—	Enter on line 7 above	If wages from **HIGHEST** paying job are—	Enter on line 7 above
0 - $50,000	$380	0 - $30,000	$380
50,001 - 100,000	700	30,001 - 60,000	700
100,001 - 130,000	780	60,001 - 110,000	780
130,001 - 230,000	900	110,001 - 230,000	900
230,001 and over	990	230,001 and over	990

Appendix E4

Form **W-5**

Department of the Treasury
Internal Revenue Service

**Earned Income Credit
Advance Payment Certificate**

19**95**

Instructions

Purpose

Use Form W-5 if you are eligible to get part of the earned income credit (EIC) in advance with your pay and choose to do so. If you choose not to get advance payments, you can still claim the EIC on your 1995 tax return.

Caution: *At the time this form went to print, Congress was considering legislation that would (1) allow certain members of the Armed Forces stationed outside the United States to claim the EIC and get advance payment of the EIC for 1995, (2) require the reporting of social security numbers for qualifying children born after November 1, 1995, and (3) make most nonresident aliens ineligible to claim the EIC for 1995. For later information about this legislation, get Pub. 553, Highlights of 1994 Tax Law Changes.*

What Is the EIC?

The EIC is a special credit for certain workers. It reduces tax you owe. It may give you a refund even if you don't owe any tax. For 1995, the EIC can be as much as $2,094 if you have one qualifying child; $3,110 if you have more than one qualifying child; $314 if you do not have a qualifying child. See **Who Is a Qualifying Child?** later. But you **cannot** get advance EIC payments unless you have a qualifying child.

Who Is Eligible To Get Advance EIC Payments?

You are eligible to get advance EIC payments if **all three** of the following apply:

1. You have at least one qualifying child.

2. You expect that your 1995 earned income and adjusted gross income will each be less than $24,396 (including your spouse's income if you expect to file a joint return).

3. You expect to be able to claim the EIC for 1995. To find out if you may be able to claim the EIC, answer the questions on page 2. If you expect to file **Form 2555**, Foreign Earned Income, or **Form 2555-EZ,** Foreign Earned Income Exclusion, for 1995, you **cannot** claim the EIC.

How Do I Get Advance EIC Payments?

If you are eligible to get advance EIC payments for 1995, you may be able to get up to $105 a month added to your take-home pay. To get advance EIC payments, fill in the Form W-5 at the bottom of this page. Then, detach it and give it to your employer. If you get advance payments, you **must** file a 1995 Form 1040A or Form 1040.

You may have only **one** Form W-5 in effect with a current employer at one time. If you and your spouse are both employed, you should file separate Forms W-5.

This Form W-5 expires on December 31, 1995. If you are eligible to get advance EIC payments for 1996, you must file a new Form W-5 next year.

Note: *You may be able to get a larger credit when you file your 1995 return. For details, see Additional Credit on page 2.*

Who Is a Qualifying Child?

Any child who meets **all three** of the following conditions is a **qualifying child:**

1. The child is your son, daughter, adopted child, stepchild, foster child, or a

descendant (for example, your grandchild) of your son, daughter, or adopted child.

Note: *An adopted child includes a child placed with you by an authorized placement agency for legal adoption even if the adoption isn't final. A foster child is any child you cared for as your own child.*

2. The child is under age 19 or a full-time student under age 24 at the end of 1995, or is permanently and totally disabled.

3. The child lives with you in the United States for more than half of 1995 (for all of 1995 if a foster child). If the child does not live with you for the required time because the child was born or died in 1995, the child is considered to have lived with you for all of 1995 if your home in the United States was the child's home for the entire time he or she was alive in 1995.

Note: *Temporary absences such as for school, medical care, or vacation count as time lived with you.*

Married child.—If the child is married at the end of 1995, the child is a qualifying child only if you may claim the child as your dependent or the following **Exception** applies to you.

Exception. You are the custodial parent and would be able to claim the child as your dependent, but the noncustodial parent claims the child as a dependent because—

• You signed **Form 8332,** Release of Claim to Exemption for Child of Divorced or Separated Parents, or a similar statement, agreeing not to claim the child for 1995, or

(Continued on page 2)

▼ *Give the lower part to your employer; keep the top part for your records.* ▼

········· Detach along this line ·········

Form **W-5**

Department of the Treasury
Internal Revenue Service

**Earned Income Credit
Advance Payment Certificate**

▶ **Give this certificate to your employer.**
▶ **This certificate expires on December 31, 1995.**

OMB No. 1545-1342

19**95**

Type or print your full name

Your social security number

Note: *If you get advance payments of the earned income credit for 1995, you **must** file a 1995 Form 1040A or Form 1040. To get advance payments, you **must** have a qualifying child and your filing status must be any status **except** married filing a separate return.*

		Yes	No
1	I expect to be able to claim the earned income credit for 1995, I do not have another Form W-5 in effect with any other current employer, and I choose to get advance EIC payments		
2	Do you have a qualifying child?		
3	Are you married?		
4	If you are married, does your spouse have a Form W-5 in effect for 1995 with any employer?		

Under penalties of perjury, I declare that the information I have furnished above is, to the best of my knowledge, true, correct, and complete.

Signature ▶   Date ▶

Cat. No. 10227P

Appendix E4　　113

Form W-5 (cont'd)

Form W-5 (1995)　　　　Page **2**

Questions To See If You May Be Able To Claim the EIC for 1995

1　Do you have a qualifying child? Read **Who Is a Qualifying Child?** on page 1 before you answer this question. If the child is married, be sure you also read **Married child** on page 1.

☐ **No. Stop here.** You may be able to claim the EIC but you **cannot** get advance EIC payments.

☐ **Yes.** Continue.

Caution: *If the child is a qualifying child for both you and another person, the child is your qualifying child only if you expect your 1995 adjusted gross income to be higher than the other person's adjusted gross income. If the other person is your spouse and you expect to file a joint return for 1995, this rule doesn't apply.*

2　Do you expect your 1995 filing status to be Married filing a separate return?

☐ **Yes. Stop here.** You **cannot** claim the EIC.

☐ **No.** Continue.

3　Do you expect that your 1995 earned income and adjusted gross income will each be less than $24,396 (less than $26,673 if you have more than one qualifying child)? If you expect to file a joint return for 1995, include your spouse's income when answering this question.

TIP: To find out what is included in adjusted gross income, you can look at page 1 of your 1994 Form 1040EZ, Form 1040A, or Form 1040.

☐ **No. Stop here.** You **cannot** claim the EIC.

☐ **Yes.** Continue. But remember, you **cannot** get advance EIC payments if you expect your 1995 earned income or adjusted gross income will be $24,396 or more.

4　Do **you** expect to be a qualifying child of another person for 1995?

☐ **No.** You may be able to claim the EIC.

☐ **Yes.** You **cannot** claim the EIC.

• You have a pre-1985 divorce decree or separation agreement that allows the noncustodial parent to claim the child and he or she gives at least $600 for the child's support in 1995.

Qualifying child of more than one person.—If the child is a qualifying child of more than one person, only the person with the **highest** adjusted gross income for 1995 may treat that child as a qualifying child. If the other person is your spouse and you expect to file a joint return for 1995, this rule doesn't apply.

Reminder.—You must get a social security number for a qualifying child born before 1995.

What If My Situation Changes?

If your situation changes after you give Form W-5 to your employer, you usually will need to file a new Form W-5. For example, you should file a new Form W-5 if any of the following applies for 1995:

• You no longer have a qualifying child. Check "No" on line 2 of your new Form W-5.

• You expect your filing status to be Married filing separately, you expect to be a qualifying child of another person, or you expect your earned income or adjusted gross income to be $24,396 or more. Check "No" on line 1 of your new Form W-5.

• You no longer want advance payments. Check "No" on line 1 of your new Form W-5.

• Your spouse files Form W-5 with his or her employer. Check "Yes" on line 4 of your new Form W-5.

Note: *If you get the EIC with your pay and find you are not eligible, you must pay it back when you file your 1995 Federal income tax return.*

Additional Information

How To Claim the EIC

If you have at least one qualifying child, fill in and attach **Schedule EIC** to your 1995 Form 1040 or Form 1040A. In addition to other information, the social security number of your qualifying child born before 1995 must be shown on Schedule EIC. To figure your EIC, use the worksheet in your 1995 Form 1040 or Form 1040A instruction booklet.

Additional Credit

You may be able to claim a larger credit when you file your 1995 tax return because your employer is not permitted to give you more than $1,257 of the EIC in advance with your pay. You may also be able to claim a larger credit if you have more than one qualifying child. But you must file your 1995 tax return to claim any additional credit.

Privacy Act and Paperwork Reduction Act Notice

We ask for the information on this form to carry out the Internal Revenue laws of the United States. Internal Revenue Code sections 3507 and 6109 and their regulations require you to provide the information requested on Form W-5 and give the form to your employer if you want advance payment of the EIC. As provided by law, we may give the information to the Department of Justice and other Federal agencies. In addition, we may give it to cities, states, and the District of Columbia so they may carry out their tax laws.

The time needed to complete this form will vary depending on individual circumstances. The estimated average time is: **Recordkeeping,** 7 min.; **Learning about the law or the form,** 9 min.; and **Preparing the form,** 26 min.

If you have comments concerning the accuracy of these time estimates or suggestions for making this form simpler, we would be happy to hear from you. You can write to both the **Internal Revenue Service,** Attention: Tax Forms Committee, PC:FP, Washington, DC 20224; and the **Office of Management and Budget,** Paperwork Reduction Project (1545-1342), Washington, DC 20503. **DO NOT** send this form to either of these offices. Instead, give it to your employer.

♻ *Printed on recycled paper*　　　　　*U.S. Government Printing Office: 1994 — 375-124*

Appendix E5

<table>
<tr><td>Form 942
(Rev. November 1994)
Department of the Treasury
Internal Revenue Service (O)</td><td>4141</td><td colspan="2">Employer's Quarterly Tax Return
for Household Employees
(For Social Security, Medicare, and Withheld Income Taxes) See separate Instructions.</td><td>OMB No. 1545-0034</td></tr>
</table>

Your name, address, employer identification number, and calendar quarter of return. (If not correct, please change.) ▶

⌐ Name

Date quarter ended ⌐

Address and ZIP code

Employer identification number

[_]

FOR IRS USE ONLY

1 1 1 1 1 1 1 1 1 1 1   2 2 2 2 2 2 2 2 2 2   3 3 3 3 3

4 4 4 5 6   7 7 7 7 7 7   8 8 8 9   10 10 10 10 10 10 10 10 10 10

If address is different from prior return, check here. ▶ ☐

Social security and Medicare taxes are due for each household employee to whom you paid cash wages of $1,000 or more in the calendar year covered by this return. For information on Federal Unemployment (FUTA) Tax, see page 3 of instructions.

If you do **NOT** expect to pay taxable wages in the future, check here . . . . ▶ ☐

1 Total cash wages subject to social security taxes (see page 1 of Instructions) .	**1**	
2 Social security taxes (multiply line 1 by 12.4% (.124))	**2**	
3 Total cash wages subject to Medicare taxes (see page 1 of Instructions) .	**3**	
4 Medicare taxes (multiply line 3 by 2.9% (.029))	**4**	
5 Federal income tax withheld (if requested by your employee) (see page 2 of Instructions) . . .	**5**	
6 Total taxes (add lines 2, 4, and 5). See instructions . . . . . . Enter the amount from line 5 of Adjustment Schedule on page 2 here ▶ $_____	**6**	
7 Advance earned income credit (EIC) payments ONLY, if any (see page 2 of Instructions) . . .	**7**	
8 Total taxes due (subtract line 7 from line 6). Pay this amount to the Internal Revenue Service. **If no tax is due, write NONE** . . . . Send Form 942 and your payment to your **Internal Revenue Service Center** (see **Where To File** on page 2 of Instructions).	**8**	

Important: You **MUST** give a Form W-2 to each employee and file Copy A with the **Social Security Administration**—see page 3 of Instructions.

Under penalties of perjury, I declare that I have examined this return, including accompanying schedules and statements, and to the best of my knowledge and belief, it is true, correct, and complete.

Signature of employer ▶

Date ▶

Cat. No. 10250E

Form **942** (Rev. 11-94)

See separate instructions for information on completing this form.

114

Form 942 (cont'd)

Form 942 (Rev. 11-94)   Page 2

Adjustment Schedule for Household Employment Taxes

Complete line 1 for each household employee for whom you paid social security and Medicare taxes for any of the first three quarters of 1994, but do not include employees to whom you paid wages of $1,000 or more during 1994.

(If you need more space, attach a separate sheet.)

1	(a) Name and social security number of household employee	(b) Total 1994 social security wages (box 3 of Form W-2)	(c) Quarter wages were paid	(d) BOTH employer's and employee's share (employee's written consent required for withheld amounts not repaid to employee)	(e) ONLY employer's share
		$	1st Quarter	$	$
	– –		2nd Quarter	$	$
			3rd Quarter	$	$
		$	1st Quarter	$	$
	– –		2nd Quarter	$	$
			3rd Quarter	$	$
		$	1st Quarter	$	$
	– –		2nd Quarter	$	$
			3rd Quarter	$	$
2	Totals.		**2**	$	$
3	Tax rate		**3**	× .153	× .0765
4	Multiply line 2 by line 3.		**4**	$	$

5   Total social security and Medicare tax adjustment. Add columns (d) and (e) of line 4 and enter the total here. Also, enter this amount in the entry space to the left of line 6 . . . .   **5** $

Employer Certification

I certify that for each employee for whom an entry is made in **column (d)**: (1) I have not withheld social security and Medicare taxes from the employee's pay, (2) I have returned to the employee any social security and Medicare taxes withheld from the employee's pay, or (3) I have obtained the employee's written consent to claim a refund on the employee's behalf of the social security and Medicare taxes withheld from the employee's pay. I also certify that for each employee for whom an entry is made in **column (e)**, either the employee would not provide written consent or I was unable to locate the employee.

Appendix E6

1994 EMPLOYEE SOCIAL SECURITY (6.2%) AND MEDICARE (1.45%) TAX DEDUCTION TABLE
(See Circular E for income tax withholding tables.)

Note: Use this table to figure the amount of social security and Medicare taxes to deduct from each wage payment. For example, on a wage payment of $180, the employee social security tax is $11.16 ($6.20 tax on $100 plus $4.96 on $80 wages). On Form 942, line 2, you report $22.32 ($180 x .124 (6.2% employee tax plus 6.2% employer tax). The employee Medicare tax is $2.61 ($1.45 tax on $100 plus $1.16 on $80 wages. On Form 942, line 4, you report $5.22 ($100 x .029 (1.45% employer tax and 1.45% employee tax).

If wage payment is:	The social security tax to be deducted is:	The Medicare tax to be deducted is:	If wage payment is:	The social security tax to be deducted is:	The Medicare tax to be deducted is:	If wage payment is:	The social security tax to be deducted is:	The Medicare tax to be deducted is:
$ 1.00	$ .06	$ .01	$36.00	$2.23	$ .52	$71.00	$4.40	$1.03
2.00	.12	.03	37.00	2.29	.54	72.00	4.46	1.04
3.00	.19	.04	38.00	2.36	.55	73.00	4.53	1.06
4.00	.25	.06	39.00	2.42	.57	74.00	4.59	1.07
5.00	.31	.07	40.00	2.48	.58	75.00	4.65	1.09
6.00	.37	.09	41.00	2.54	.59	76.00	4.71	1.10
7.00	.43	.10	42.00	2.60	.61	77.00	4.77	1.12
8.00	.50	.12	43.00	2.67	.62	78.00	4.84	1.13
9.00	.56	.13	44.00	2.73	.64	79.00	4.90	1.15
10.00	.62	.15	45.00	2.79	.65	80.00	4.96	1.16
11.00	.68	.16	46.00	2.85	.67	81.00	5.02	1.17
12.00	.74	.17	47.00	2.91	.68	82.00	5.08	1.19
13.00	.81	.19	48.00	2.98	.70	83.00	5.15	1.20
14.00	.87	.20	49.00	3.04	.71	84.00	5.21	1.22
15.00	.93	.22	50.00	3.10	.73	85.00	5.27	1.23
16.00	.99	.23	51.00	3.16	.74	86.00	5.33	1.25
17.00	1.05	.25	52.00	3.22	.75	87.00	5.39	1.26
18.00	1.12	.26	53.00	3.29	.77	88.00	5.46	1.28
19.00	1.18	.28	54.00	3.35	.78	89.00	5.52	1.29
20.00	1.24	.29	55.00	3.41	.80	90.00	5.58	1.31
21.00	1.30	.30	56.00	3.47	.81	91.00	5.64	1.32
22.00	1.36	.32	57.00	3.53	.83	92.00	5.70	1.33
23.00	1.43	.33	58.00	3.60	.84	93.00	5.77	1.35
24.00	1.49	.35	59.00	3.66	.86	94.00	5.83	1.36
25.00	1.55	.36	60.00	3.72	.87	95.00	5.89	1.38
26.00	1.61	.38	61.00	3.78	.88	96.00	5.95	1.39
27.00	1.67	.39	62.00	3.84	.90	97.00	6.01	1.41
28.00	1.74	.41	63.00	3.91	.91	98.00	6.08	1.42
29.00	1.80	.42	64.00	3.97	.93	99.00	6.14	1.44
30.00	1.86	.44	65.00	4.03	.94	100.00	6.20	1.45
31.00	1.92	.45	66.00	4.09	.96			
32.00	1.98	.46	67.00	4.15	.97			
33.00	2.05	.48	68.00	4.22	.99			
34.00	2.11	.49	69.00	4.28	1.00			
35.00	2.17	.51	70.00	4.34	1.02			

• A substitute Form W-2 with the same EIC information on the back of the employee's copy that is on Copy C of the IRS Form W-2;

• Notice 797, Possible Federal Tax Refund Due to the Earned Income Credit (EIC); or

• Your own written statement with the same wording as Notice 797.

Generally, you must give your employees direct notice about the EIC by February 7, 1995. For specific instructions about the notification requirements, see Circular E and Notice 1015, Employers—Have You Told Your Employees About the Earned Income Credit (EIC)? Notice 1015 and Notice 797 are included in this package. You can also get them by calling 1-800-TAX-FORM (1-800-829-3676).

Rounding off to whole dollars.—You may round off cash wages paid to the nearest whole dollar to determine the $1,000 test, figure employee tax deductions, and report wages on your return. For example, if you paid from $104.50 to $105.49, you may

report $105 as the taxable wage. If you choose the rounding method, use it consistently for all wage payments to household employees in that quarter

Additional Information

You can get the following forms and publications by calling 1-800-TAX-FORM (1-800-829-3676).

Pub. 15, Circular E, Employer's Tax Guide

Pub. 51, Circular A, Agricultural Employer's Tax Guide

Pub. 926, Employment Taxes for Household Employers

Form W-2, Wage and Tax Statement

Form W-3, Transmittal of Wage and Tax Statements

Form W-4, Employee's Withholding Allowance Certificate

Form W-5, Earned Income Credit Advance Payment Certificate

Notice 576, Notice to Household Employers About Federal Unemployment Taxes

Notice 587, Preparing Form W-2 for Your Household Employee

Notice 797, Possible Federal Tax Refund Due to the Earned Income Credit (EIC)

Notice 1015, Employers—Have You Told Your Employees About the Earned Income Credit (EIC)?

Form 940 and Form 940-EZ, Employer's Annual Federal Unemployment (FUTA) Tax Return

Form 941, Employer's Quarterly Federal Tax Return

Form 943, Employer's Annual Tax Return for Agricultural Employees

Page 4

Appendix E7

Form **940-EZ**

Department of the Treasury
Internal Revenue Service (O)

**Employer's Annual Federal
Unemployment (FUTA) Tax Return**

OMB No. 1545-1110

19**94**

Name (as distinguished from trade name)	Calendar year	T
		FF
		FD
Trade name, if any		FP
		I
Address and ZIP code	Employer identification number	T

Follow the chart under **Who May Use Form 940-EZ** on page 2. If you cannot use Form 940-EZ, you must use Form 940 instead.

A   Enter the amount of contributions paid to your state unemployment fund. (See instructions for line A on page 4.)▶ $ ....

B   (1) Enter the name of the state where you have to pay contributions . . . . ▶   ....
    (2) Enter your state reporting number as shown on state unemployment tax return. ▶

If you will not have to file returns in the future, check here (see Who Must File, on page 2) complete, and sign the return . . . . . . ▶ ☐

If this is an Amended Return check here . . . . ▶ ☐

Part I **Taxable Wages and FUTA Tax**

1	Total payments (including payments shown on lines 2 and 3) during the calendar year for services of employees	1	
		Amount paid	
2	Exempt payments. (Explain all exempt payments, attaching additional sheets if necessary.) ▶	2	
3	Payments for services of more than $7,000. Enter only amounts over the first $7,000 paid to each employee. Do not include any exempt payments from line 2. Do not use your state wage limitation. The $7,000 amount is the Federal wage base. Your state wage base may be different	3	
4	Total exempt payments (add lines 2 and 3)	4	
5	Total taxable wages (subtract line 4 from line 1) . . . . ▶	5	
6	FUTA tax. Multiply the wages on line 5 by .008 and enter here. (If the result is over $100, also complete Part II.) .	6	
7	Total FUTA tax deposited for the year, including any overpayment applied from a prior year (from your records) .	7	
8	Amount you owe (subtract line 7 from line 6). This should be $100 or less. Pay to "Internal Revenue Service." ▶	8	
9	Overpayment (subtract line 6 from line 7). Check if it is to be: ☐ Applied to next return, or ☐ Refunded ▶	9	

Part II **Record of Quarterly Federal Unemployment Tax Liability** (Do not include state liability.) Complete only if line 6 is over $100.

Quarter	First (Jan. 1 – Mar. 31)	Second (Apr. 1 – June 30)	Third (July 1 – Sept. 30)	Fourth (Oct. 1 – Dec. 31)	Total for year
Liability for quarter					

Under penalties of perjury, I declare that I have examined this return, including accompanying schedules and statements, and, to the best of my knowledge and belief, it is true, correct, and complete, and that no part of any payment made to a state unemployment fund claimed as a credit was, or is to be, deducted from the payments to employees

Signature ▶   Title (Owner, etc.) ▶   Date ▶

Cat. No. 10983G

Form **940-EZ** (1994

DO NOT DETACH

Form **940-V-EZ**

Department of the Treasury
Internal Revenue Service

Form 940-EZ Payment Voucher

19**94**

Complete boxes 1, 2, 6, and 7. **Do not send cash and do not staple your payment to this voucher.** Make your check or money order, with your employer identification number clearly written on it, payable to the **Internal Revenue Service.**

1 Your employer identification number	2 Enter the first four letters of your business name	3 MFT	4 Tax year	5 Transaction code
		1 0	9 4 1 2	6 1 0
	6 Your name and address		7 Amount of payment	
Do not staple your payment to this voucher.			$	Do not send cash.

Appendix E8

Form 940

Department of the Treasury
Internal Revenue Service (O)

Employer's Annual Federal Unemployment (FUTA) Tax Return

► For Paperwork Reduction Act Notice, see separate instructions.

1994

T	
FF	
FD	
FP	
I	
T	

Name (as distinguished from trade name)   Calendar year

Trade name, if any

Address and ZIP code   Employer identification number

A   Are you required to pay unemployment contributions to only one state? (If no, skip questions B and C.)   ☐ Yes   ☐ No

B   Did you pay all state unemployment contributions by January 31, 1995? (If a 0% experience rate is granted, check "Yes.") (If no, skip question C.)   ☐ Yes   ☐ No

C   Were all wages that were taxable for FUTA tax also taxable for your state's unemployment tax?   ☐ Yes   ☐ No

If you answered "No" to any of these questions, you must file Form 940. If you answered "Yes" to all the questions, you may file Form 940-EZ, which is a simplified version of Form 940. You can get Form 940-EZ by calling 1-800-TAX-FORM (1-800-829-3676).

If you will not have to file returns in the future, check here, complete, and sign the return   ► ☐
If this is an Amended Return, check here   ► ☐

Part I   Computation of Taxable Wages

1	Total payments (including exempt payments) during the calendar year for services of employees.	**1**	
2	Exempt payments. (Explain each exemption shown, attach additional sheets if necessary.) ►	Amount paid **2**	
3	Payments of more than $7,000 for services. Enter only amounts over the first $7,000 paid to each employee. Do not include payments from line 2. The $7,000 amount is the Federal wage base. Your state wage base may be different. **Do not use the state wage limitation**	**3**	
4	Total exempt payments (add lines 2 and 3).	**4**	
5	**Total taxable wages (subtract line 4 from line 1)** ►	**5**	

Be sure to complete both sides of this return and sign in the space provided on the back.   Cat. No. 11234O   Form **940** (1994)

DO NOT DETACH

Form 940-V

Department of the Treasury
Internal Revenue Service

Form 940 Payment Voucher

1994

Complete boxes 1, 2, 6, and 7. Do not send cash and do not staple your payment to this voucher. Make your check or money order payable to the Internal Revenue Service. If tax due is over $100, make the deposit with Form 8109.

1 Your employer identification number	2 Enter the first four letters of your business name	3 MFT	4 Tax year	5 Transaction code
		1 0	9 4 1 2	6 1 0
	6 Your business name and address		7 Amount of payment	
			$	
Do not staple your payment to this voucher.			Do not send cash.	

120

Form 940 (cont'd)

Form 940 (1994) Page **2**

Part II   **Tax Due or Refund**

1	Gross FUTA tax. Multiply the wages in Part I, line 5, by .062	**1**	
2	Maximum credit. Multiply the wages in Part I, line 5, by .054	**2**	
3	Computation of tentative credit (Note: *All taxpayers must complete the applicable columns.*)		

(a) Name of state	(b) State reporting number(s) as shown on employer's state contribution returns	(c) Taxable payroll (as defined in state act)	(d) State experience rate period		(e) State experience rate	(f) Contributions if rate had been 5.4% (col. (c) x .054)	(g) Contributions payable at experience rate (col. (c) x col. (e))	(h) Additional credit (col. (f) minus col.(g)). If 0 or less, enter -0-.	(i) Contributions actually paid to state
			From	To					

3a	Totals . . . . ▶		
3b	Total tentative credit (add line 3a, columns (h) and (i) only—see instructions for limitations on late payments) ▶		
4			
5			
6	Credit: Enter the smaller of the amount in Part II, line 2, or line 3b	**6**	
7	Total FUTA tax (subtract line 6 from line 1)	**7**	
8	Total FUTA tax deposited for the year, including any overpayment applied from a prior year . .	**8**	
9	Balance due (subtract line 8 from line 7). This should be $100 or less. Pay to the Internal Revenue Service. See page 3 of the Instructions for Form 940 for details . . . . ▶	**9**	
10	Overpayment (subtract line 7 from line 8). Check if it is to be: ☐ Applied to next return, or ☐ Refunded . . . . ▶	**10**	

Part III   **Record of Quarterly Federal Unemployment Tax Liability** *(Do not include state liability)*

Quarter	First	Second	Third	Fourth	Total for year
Liability for quarter					

Under penalties of perjury, I declare that I have examined this return, including accompanying schedules and statements, and to the best of my knowledge and belief, it is true, correct, and complete, and that no part of any payment made to a state unemployment fund claimed as a credit was or is to be deducted from the payments to employees.

Signature ▶   Title (Owner, etc.) ▶   Date ▶

Appendix E9

Department of the Treasury
Internal Revenue Service (O)

Child and Dependent Care Expenses

▶ Attach to Form 1040.

▶ See separate instructions.

OMB No. 1545-0068

1994

Attachment
Sequence No. **21**

Name(s) shown on Form 1040

Your social security number

You need to understand the following terms to complete this form:
Qualifying Person(s), Dependent Care Benefits, Qualified Expenses, and **Earned Income.** See **Important Terms** on page 1 of the Form 2441 instructions.

Part I Persons or Organizations Who Provided the Care—You must complete this part. (If you need more space, use the bottom of page 2.)

1	(a) Care provider's name	(b) Address (number, street, apt. no., city, state, and ZIP code)	(c) Identifying number (SSN or EIN)	(d) Amount paid (see instructions)

2   Add the amounts in column (d) of line 1 . . . . **2**

3   Enter the number of qualifying persons cared for in 1994 . . . . ▶ [ ]

Did you receive dependent care benefits?	NO ──▶ Complete only Part II below.
	YES ──▶ Complete Part III on the back now.

Part II Credit for Child and Dependent Care Expenses

4   Enter the amount of **qualified expenses** you incurred and paid in 1994. DO NOT enter more than $2,400 for one qualifying person or $4,800 for two or more persons. If you completed Part III, enter the amount from line 25 . . . . **4**

5   Enter YOUR **earned income** **5**

6   If married filing a joint return, enter YOUR SPOUSE'S earned income (if student or disabled, see the instructions); **all others,** enter the amount from line 5 . . . . **6**

7   Enter the **smallest** of line 4, 5, or 6 . . . . **7**

8   Enter the amount from Form 1040, line 32 . . . . **8**

9   Enter on line 9 the decimal amount shown below that applies to the amount on line 8

If line 8 is—		Decimal amount is	If line 8 is—		Decimal amount is
Over	But not over		Over	But not over	
$0—10,000		.30	$20,000—22,000		.24
10,000—12,000		.29	22,000—24,000		.23
12,000—14,000		.28	24,000—26,000		.22
14,000—16,000		.27	26,000—28,000		.21
16,000—18,000		.26	28,000—No limit		.20
18,000—20,000		.25			

9 ×.

10   Multiply **line 7** by the decimal amount on line 9. Enter the result. Then, see the instructions for the amount of credit to enter on Form 1040, line 41 . . . . **10**
   Caution: *If you paid $50 or more in a calendar quarter to a person who worked in your home, you must file an employment tax return. Get Form 942 for details.*

For Paperwork Reduction Act Notice, see separate instructions.   Cat. No. 11862M   Form **2441** (1994)

Form 2441 (cont'd)

Form 2441 (1994) Page **2**

Part III **Dependent Care Benefits**—Complete this part **only** if you received these benefits.

11   Enter the total amount of **dependent care benefits** you received for 1994. This amount should be shown in box 10 of your W-2 form(s). DO NOT include amounts that were reported to you as wages in box 1 of Form(s) W-2 . . . .   **11**

12   Enter the amount forfeited, if any. See the instructions **12**

13   Subtract line 12 from line 11 . . . .   **13**

14   Enter the total amount of **qualified expenses** incurred in 1994 for the care of the qualifying person(s) **14**

15   Enter the **smaller** of line 13 or 14 . . . .   **15**

16   Enter YOUR **earned income** **16**

17   If married filing a joint return, enter YOUR SPOUSE'S earned income (if student or disabled, see the line 6 instructions); if married filing a separate return, see the instructions for the amount to enter; **all others**, enter the amount from line 16 . .   **17**

18   Enter the **smallest** of line 15, 16, or 17. . . . .   **18**

19   **Excluded benefits.** Enter here the **smaller** of the following:

    • The amount from line 18, or
    • $5,000 ($2,500 if married filing a separate return and you were required to enter your spouse's earned income on line 17). **19**

20   **Taxable benefits.** Subtract line 19 from line 13. Also, include this amount on Form 1040, line 7. On the dotted line next to line 7, write "DCB" **20**

To claim the child and dependent care credit, complete lines 21–25 below, and lines 4–10 on the front of this form.

21   Enter the amount of qualified expenses you incurred and paid in 1994. DO NOT include on this line any excluded benefits shown on line 19 . . . .   **21**

22   Enter $2,400 ($4,800 if two or more qualifying persons) . . .   **22**

23   Enter the amount from line 19 . . . .   **23**

24   Subtract line 23 from line 22. If zero or less, **STOP.** You cannot take the credit. **Exception.** If you paid 1993 expenses in 1994, see the line 10 instructions **24**

25   Enter the **smaller** of line 21 or 24 here and on line 4 on the front of this form **25**

    ♻ *Printed on recycled paper*   *U.S. Government Printing Office: 1994 — 375-345*

Appendix E10

Appendix F

U.S. Department of Justice
Immigration and Naturalization Service

OMB No. 1115-0136
Employment Eligibility Verification

Please read instructions carefully before completing this form. The instructions must be available during completion of this form. ANTI-DISCRIMINATION NOTICE. It is illegal to discriminate against work eligible individuals. Employers CANNOT specify which document(s) they will accept from an employee. The refusal to hire an individual because of a future expiration date may also constitute illegal discrimination.

Section 1. Employee Information and Verification. To be completed and signed by employee at the time employment begins

Print Name: Last	First	Middle Initial	Maiden Name

Address (Street Name and Number)	Apt. #	Date of Birth (month/day/year)

City	State	Zip Code	Social Security #

I am aware that federal law provides for imprisonment and/or fines for false statements or use of false documents in connection with the completion of this form.

I attest, under penalty of perjury, that I am (check one of the following):
☐ A citizen or national of the United States
☐ A Lawful Permanent Resident (Alien # A_____)
☐ An alien authorized to work until___/___/___
(Alien # or Admission # _____)

Employee's Signature	Date (month/day/year)

Preparer and/or Translator Certification. (To be completed and signed if Section 1 is prepared by a person other than the employee.) I attest, under penalty of perjury, that I have assisted in the completion of this form and that to the best of my knowledge the information is true and correct.

Preparer's/Translator's Signature	Print Name

Address (Street Name and Number, City, State, Zip Code)	Date (month/day/year)

Section 2. Employer Review and Verification. To be completed and signed by employer. Examine one document from List A OR examine one document from List B and one from List C as listed on the reverse of this form and record the title, number and expiration date, if any, of the document(s)

List A	OR	List B	AND	List C
Document title: _____		_____		_____
Issuing authority: _____		_____		_____
Document #: _____		_____		_____
Expiration Date (if any): ___/___/___		___/___/___		___/___/___
Document #: _____				
Expiration Date (if any): ___/___/___				

CERTIFICATION - I attest, under penalty of perjury, that I have examined the document(s) presented by the above-named employee, that the above-listed document(s) appear to be genuine and to relate to the employee named, that the employee began employment on (month/day/year) ___/___/___ and that to the best of my knowledge the employee is eligible to work in the United States. (State employment agencies may omit the date the employee began employment).

Signature of Employer or Authorized Representative	Print Name	Title

Business or Organization Name	Address (Street Name and Number, City, State, Zip Code)	Date (month/day/year)

Section 3. Updating and Reverification. To be completed and signed by employer

A. New Name (if applicable)	B. Date of rehire (month/day/year) (if applicable)

C. If employee's previous grant of work authorization has expired, provide the information below for the document that establishes current employment eligibility.

Document Title: _____ Document #: _____ Expiration Date (if any): ___/___/___

I attest, under penalty of perjury, that to the best of my knowledge, this employee is eligible to work in the United States, and if the employee presented document(s), the document(s) I have examined appear to be genuine and to relate to the individual.

Signature of Employer or Authorized Representative	Date (month/day/year)

Form I-9 (Rev. 11-21-91) N

Appendix G

CHILD CARE PLACEMENT AGENCIES AND SERVICES IN THE UNITED STATES

Alabama

Birmingham Home Services, Inc.
Office Park Circle, Building 16, Suite 4
Birmingham, AL 35223
205–871–2032
Registration: $100;
  fee: $200 to $600

Companions & Sitters
115 Sally Lane
Madison, AL 35758
205–772–8246

Companions Sitter
  Service
Headline, AL 36345
205–693–5525

Home Buddies
1000 Airport Road,
  Suite 11
Huntsville, AL 35802
205–882–1200
Fee: $300

Arkansas

Granny's and Nanny's
410 Conway Street
Benton, AR 72015
501–776–2664
Fee: varies

Nannies for You
7624 Cantrell
Little Rock, AR 72207
501–228–6264

Arizona

Helping Hand
5656 West College
Phoenix, AZ 85031
602–846–5908

Nanny Finders
Phoenix, AZ 85018
602–952–2500

California

American Nanny Plan
4650 Arrow Highway,
    Suite A-10
Montclair, CA 91763
909–624–7711
Registration: $25,
    fee: 10 percent of nan-
    ny's annual salary

Au Pair Extraordinaire
Granda Hills, CA 91344
818–366–4420

Au Pair Extraordinaire
6105 West 6th Street
Los Angeles, CA 90048
818–831–9032
Registration: $150;
    fee: one month of nan-
    ny's salary

Aunt Ann's Agency
760 Market, No. 539
San Francisco, CA 94102
415–421–8442
Fee: 75 percent of nan-
    ny's monthly salary

Baby Buddies Agency,
    Inc.
144 South Beverly Drive
Beverly Hills, CA 90212
310–273–2330
Fee: 10 percent of nan-
    ny's annual salary

Baby Nurses, Ltd.
11941 Wilshire Boule-
    vard, No. 26
Los Angeles, CA 90025
310–477–3812

Bay Area Second Mom
644 Towle Place
Palo Alto, CA 94306
415–858–2469
Fee: $1,200

Be in Our Care
31 La Mesa Lane
Walnut Creek, CA 94589
510–933–2273
Fee: one month of nan-
    ny's salary

Buckingham Nannies
14542 Venture Boule-
vard, Suite 2008
Sherman Oaks, CA
91423
818-784-6504

California Nanny
310 Sun Stream Street
Danville, CA 94506
510-449-1071
Fee: varies

Dial a Mom, Inc.
2659 Towngate Road,
No. 108
Westlake Village, CA
91361
805-496-2264
Fee: 70 percent of nan-
ny's monthly salary

Fairfield Nanny Service
10061 Talbert Avenue,
Suite 202
Fountain Valley, CA
92708
714-965-5642
Fee: one month of nan-
ny's salary

The Governess Agency
125 East Baker Street
Costa Mesa, CA 92626
714-979-6200

The Governess Agency
3111 Camino Del Rio
North
San Diego, CA 92108
619-528-2244

The Governess Agency
4655 Cass, No. 405 R
San Diego, CA 92109
619-270-8311
Fee: one month of nan-
ny's salary

Here's Help 1, Inc.
3251 Sacramento Street
San Francisco, CA 94115
415-563-0242
Fee: 75 percent of nan-
ny's monthly salary

I Love My Nanny
1072 South Saratoga
Vale Road, Suite 13203
San Jose, CA 95129
408-99-NANNY
Fee: varies

K&D Domestic Agency
7710 Balboa Avenue
San Diego, CA 92123
619-296-0432
Fee: one month of nan-
ny's salary

Maid in America
30 North Raymond Avenue, No. 406
Pasadena, CA 91103
818–792–9958

Malibu Mamas Agency
22525 Pacific Coast Highway, Suite 203
Malibu, CA 90265
310–456–8113
Fee: 10 percent of nanny's annual salary

Mom Away
1015 Keith Avenue
Berkeley, CA 94708
510–559–9395
Fee: one month of nanny's salary

Mommyworks, Inc.
24331 Murilands Boulevard, No. E
Lake Forest, CA 92630
714–830–9997
Registration: $50; fee: $700

Mother's Helper Agency
9454 Wilshire Boulevard, No. 600
Beverly Hills, CA 90212
800–942–2278;
310–271–1159
Registration: $250; fee: $1,000

Mother's Indeed
425 Sherman Avenue, Suite 130
Palo Alto, CA 94306
415–326–8570

My Nannie Referral
2082 Michelson
Irvine, CA 92715
714–660–8555
Fee: varies

Nannies Care
2701 Adrian Street
San Diego, CA 92110
619–222–2490
Registration: $250; fee: $900

Nannies Limited
1250 Kay Lane
Oakley, CA 94561
510–625–8382
Fee: one month of nanny's salary

Nannies Unlimited Agency
321 South Beverly Drive, No. 204
Beverly Hills, CA 90212
213–551–1621
Fee: one month of nanny's salary

Newport Nanny Place-
ment Agency
18582 Beach Boulevard,
Suite 222
Huntington Beach, CA
92648
714–968–0380

North County Nannies
P.O. Box 460339
Escondido, CA 92046
619–480-0500
Fee: $1,000 minimum for
live-in, $500 minimum
for live-out

Prestige Nanny Service
P.O. Box 921538
Sylmar, CA 91392
818–364–6144
Registration: $25;
fee: not specified

Rent a Parent Personnel
Services
98 Main Street, Suite 504
Triburon, CA 94920
415–435–2642
Fee: one month of nan-
ny's salary

Rose's Domestic Agency
6105 West 6th Street
Los Angeles, CA 90048
213–937–3196
Fee: one month of nan-
ny's salary

TLC, Inc.
5424–10 Sunol Boule-
vard, Suite 111
Pleasanton, CA 94566
510–426–8028
Fee: one month of nan-
ny's salary

Colorado

First Choice Nanny
9725 East Hampton
Aurora, CO 80014
303–368–0299

National Nannies
1681 South Dayton
Street
Denver, CO 80231
303–333–6264

Rent a Mom of Colo-
rado, Inc.
360 South Monroe, Suite
310
Denver, CO 80209
303–322–1399
Registration: $75;
fee: $600 to $800

Starkey and Associates,
Inc.
1410 High Street
Denver, CO 80218
303–394–4908
Fee: varies

Town and Country Nan-
nies, Inc.
2384 South Broadway
Denver, CO 80210
305–744–6112
Registration: $150;
fee: varies

Connecticut

Ascot Nannies of
Greater New York,
Inc.
28 Lafayette Place
Greenwich, CT 06830
203–629–2200
Fee: $1,400

Care for Kids, Inc.
P.O. Box 27
Rowayton, CT 06853
203–838–7356
Fee: $1,500

Connecticut Nanny, Inc.
P.O. Box 931
Litchfield, CT 06840
203–966–9737
Registration: $25;
fee: 12 percent of nan-
ny's annual salary

Family Extensions
244 Elm Street
New Canaan, CT 06840
203–966–9737
Registration: $25;
fee: 12 percent of nan-
ny's annual salary

Help!
15 Bridge Road
Weston, CT 06883
203–226–3456;
203–226–HELP
Fee: one month of nan-
ny's salary, minimum
$1,400

Help Mates Unlimited
3 Terrace Drive
Bethel, CT 06801
800–LIVE-INS;
203–274–7511
Registration: $125;
fee: $999

Help Place Nanny
Bridge Road
Weston, CT 06883
203–226–4200

Helping Hands
(Childcare Connection)
P.O. Box 237
Greenwich, CT 06836
800–544–NANI
Fee: $1,850

Namely Nannies
74 Greenwich Avenue
Greenwich, CT 06830
203–629–8775
Fee: $1,000

Nannies Source, Inc.
P.O. Box 7371
Wilton, CT 06897
800–322–6264;
203–762–9004
Fee: $1,000

Nanny Concern, Inc.
15 Mountain Road
Wilton, CT 06897
203–544–9462
Fee: $1,400

Parents Choice
100 Mill Plain Road
Danbury, CT 06811
203–791–3891
Registration: $100; fee:
  $800

TGIF Peopleworks
P.O. Box 828
Old Lyme, CT 06371
203–434–2526

District of Columbia

Au Pair Homestay, USA
1015 Fifteenth Street,
  N.W., Suite 750

Washington, DC 20005
202–408–5380
Registration: $75;
  fee: not available

Delaware

A Choice Nanny
11 Continental Drive,
  108
Newark, DE 19713
302–292–0626
Fee: varies

Florida

Baby Sitters Agency Bu-
  reau and Registry
103 Windy Place
Brandon, FL 33511
813–681–2002
Fee: $5.50 an hour, mini-
  mum of four hours,
  plus $3 transportation
  charge

A Choice Nanny
7232 Sand Lake Road,
  Suite 305
Orlando, FL 32819
407–876–1666
Fee: $100 to $1,200

A Choice Nanny
1413 South Howard Avenue, Suite 201
Tampa, FL 33606
813–254–8687
Fee: $100 to $1,200

Dial a Sitter, Inc.
1665 Spring Ridge Circle
Wintergarden, FL 34787
800–472–7121;
407–877–6388
Registration: $60;
  fee: $240

Distinctive Domestic, Inc.
3000 East Sunrise Boulevard, No. 5E
Fort Lauderdale, FL 33304
305–564–8229
Registration: $150;
  fee: $250 to $750

House Sitters
8619 Shauna Oaks Circle
  North
Jacksonville, FL 32211
904–745–5252

Mother's Care Referral
  Service, Inc.
313 South Ketch Drive
Fort Lauderdale, FL
  33326
305–384–7141
Registration: $50; fee:
  $250

Mother's Helpmates
813 East Bloomingdale
  Avenue, Suite 160
Brandon, FL 33511
813–681–5183
Registration: $150;
  fee: $650 to $1,500

Nannies for Hire, Inc.
430 Southwest 169th
  Terrace
Fort Lauderdale, FL
  33326
305–932–5335

Nannies Who Care, Inc.
1436 Dinnerbell Lane
  East
Dunedin, FL 34698
813–736–4295
Registration: $75;
  fee: $425–$625–$725

Nanny Care, Inc.
6315 Presidential Court,
  Suite D
Fort Myers, FL 33919
800–728–2236;
  813–433–1909
Registration: $150

Nanny Network, Inc.
20145 Northeast Avenue
Miami, FL 33180
305–932–5335
Registration: $150;
  fee: $1,250

Nanny's Sitters, Inc.
252 Ewing Court, N.W.
Fort Walton, FL 32548
904–862–9652

Georgia

A Friend of the Family
895 Mount Vernon
  Highway
Atlanta, GA 30327
404–255–2848
Fee: $750 to $2,300

Nannies From ESP
  Inc.,
Employment Search
  Professionals
533 North Highway 29
Newnan, GA 30263
404–253–9354
Registration: $75;
  fee: 9 percent of
  nanny's annual
  salary

National Nanny
  Network
6065 Roswell Road,
  Suite 632
Atlanta, GA 30328
404–262–2585

TLC Sitters of Atlanta,
  Inc.
1262 Concord Road
Smyna, GA 30080
708–435–6250
Registration: $150;
  fee: varies

Iowa

American Nanny Plus
700 Locust, Suite 104
Des Moines, IA 50309
515–245–4279
Registration: varies

Illinois

Care for Kids, Inc.
1207 Glencoe Avenue
Highland Park, IL
  60035–4007
708–433–4737
Fee: 10 percent of nan-
  ny's annual salary or
  $10 a day for tempo-
  rary help

Child Care of Dupage,
  Inc.
27 West 170 Sycamore
Winfield, IL 60190
708–665–7007
Fee: $750 to $900

Childminders, Inc.
4350 Oakton, Suite 204
Skokie, IL 60076
708–673–8998
Fee: $900

Nannies Network
2914 North Sheffield
Chicago, IL 60657
312–528–4949

Nannies of DuPage, Inc.
P.O. Box 2368
Darien, IL 60559
708–963–6311
Fee: $950

Nannies Sitters, Inc.
2200 West Highs Road
Schaumburg, IL 60195
708–885–1700

Nanny
1342 West Cornel
Chicago, IL 60657
312–549–0410

Nanny Sitting Service
103 Furn Drive
Island Lake, IL 60042
708–526–2853

Nanny's Nook
127 South Main Street
Galena, IL 61036
815–777–0232

R&R Domestic Agency
280 Sylvan
Glencoe, IL 60022
708–835–2525
Fee: one week of nan-
    ny's salary

Indiana

Nannies of Indiana
8550 East Washington
Indianapolis, IN 46229
317–897–6767

Nanny Search
52130 South Lakeshore
    Drive
Granger, IN 46530
219–277–8090
Registration: $35 for tem-
    porary help,
$75 for permanent help;
    fee: $500

Kansas

English Nannie
6800 West 93rd Street
Shawnee, KS 66212
913–341–5812

Kentucky

Private Nanny
S.E. 117 Madison
  Avenue
Bardstow, KY 40004
502–348–6228

Temporary Nanny
3361 Commodore
Lexington, KY 40502
606–266–5403

Louisiana

Dependable Nursing
  and Family Care, Inc.
101 West Robert E. Lee,
  Suite 201
New Orleans, LA 70124
800–862–5806;
504–282–2200
Fee: $1,200

Massachusetts

ABC Nannies
2 Locust Lane
Watertown, MA 02172
617–923–0605

Au Pair Professionals of
  Boston
135 Selwyn Road
Newton, MA 02161
617–527–0114
Fee: $1,400

Baby Sitting Placement
  Service
1550 Worcester Road
Framingham, MA 01715
508–872–8428

Beacon Hill Nannies,
  Inc.
440 Commercial Street
Boston, MA 02109
617–227–5592
Fee: $125 to $375

Child Care Placement
  Service, Inc.
149 Buckminster Road
Brookline, MA 02146
617–566–3657
Fee: varies

EF Au Pair
1 Memorial Drive
Cambridge, MA 02142
800–333–6056;
617–252–6145
Registration: $175;
  fee: $3,190

The Minute Women
111 Union Wharf, No. A
Boston, MA 02109
617–227–1889

The Minute Women
49 Waltham Street
Lexington, MA 02173
617–862–3300

Nannie for Rent
1 Scribner Road
Peabody, MA 01960
508–535–0127

Nannies Nook, Inc.
3 Wanders Drive
Hingham, MA 02043
800–542–4397;
617–749–8097
Registration: $75;
  fee: $950 to $1,350

Nanny Connection
11 Anderson
Georgetown, MA 01833
508–352–7653

Original Nanny Service
172 Institute Road
Worcester, MA 01602
508–755–9284
Registration: $75;
  fee: $1,100

Yankee Sitters
P.O. Box 475
Webster, MA 01570
508–949–6244
Registration: $75;
  fee: $800

Maryland

B&C Regal Domestic,
  Inc.
P.O. Box 34557
Bethesda, MD 20817
301–469–6817
Fee: 9 percent to 12 per-
  cent of nanny's annual
  salary

Best Nanny Employment
  Agency, Inc.
1496 Registertown Road,
  Suite 108
Baltimore, MD 21208
410–486–2135
Registration: $100;
  fee: $1,200

Capable Care of Mary-
  land, Inc.
5100 Ridgefield Road,
  No. 212
Bethesda, MD 20816
301–718–3700
Registration: $50;
  fee: not specified

A Choice Nanny
2530 Riva Road
Annapolis, MD 21401
410–730–2356

A Choice Nanny
8827 Columbia 100 Park-
way, Suite 1A
Columbia, MD 21204
410–823–8687
Registration: $100;
fee: $1,000 to $1,200

A Choice Nanny
7300 York Road, Suite
101
Towson, MD 21204
410–823–8687
Registration: $100;
fee: $1,000 to $1,200

A Gentle Touch Nanny
311 Eldwood Court
Annapolis, MD 21401
301–858–7140
Fee: varies

Potomac Nannies, Ltd.
7315 Wisconsin Avenue,
Suite 3231
West Bethesda, MD
20814
301–986–0048
Registration: $75;
fee: $700

Sterling Nannies, Inc.
10008 Rogart Road
Silver Spring, MD 20901
301–593–0069
Registration: $50;
fee: $1,000

White House Nannies,
Inc.
4733 Bethesda Avenue,
Suite 804
Bethesda, MD 20814
301–654–5506

Maine

Exclusively Nannies
P.O. Box 1068
West Brook, ME 04092
207–871–8227
Registration: $15;
fee: $600

Michigan

Nanny
216 First Street
Rochester, MI 48307
810–650–8454

Nanny Connection
233 East Fulton
Grand Rapids, MI 49503
616–456–5151

The Nanny Corporation
325 East Eisenhower
  Parkway, Suite 106
Ann Arbor, MI 48108
313–769–5265;
313–258–6330
Registration: $150;
  fee: $975 to $1,075

Nannies of America
4190 Telegraph, Suite
  3300
Bloomfield Hills, MI
  48302
313–540–4960
Fee: varies

Poppin's Agency for
  Nannies
P.O. Box 361025
Grosse Pointe, MI 48236
313–884–9118

Your Nannies
  Association
Farmington, MI 48334
810–851–1620

Minnesota

C&I Nanny Professionals
245 East 6th Street, Suite
  703
St. Paul, MN 55101
612–221–0587
Registration: $100;
  fee: $950

Minnesota Nannies
8854 Jasmine
Eden Prairie, MN 55344
612–941–0256

Nannies from the
  Heartland
5490 Balsam Lane
Minneapolis, MN 55442
612–550–0219
Registration: $100;
  fee: $750 to $850

Parents Partners Line,
  Inc.
2 Appletree Square,
  Suite 134
Bloomington, MN 55425
612–854–8594
Registration: $100;
  fee: $800

Patty's School Place-
  ments, Inc.
5213 Winchester Lane
Minneapolis, MN 55429
612–533–5219
Registration: $100;
  fee: $850

Umbrella Child Care
  Services
3508 West 22nd Street
Minneapolis, MN 55416
612–929–0877
Registration: $60 to $180;
  fee: $300 to $900

Missouri

Ashford Nannies
P.O. Box 22529
Kansas City, MO 64113
816–444–5059
Fee: not specified

Friend of the Family of
  Kansas City
12414 Summit Street
Kansas City, MO 64145
406–542–0241
Registration: $400 to
  $450

House Sitters
1045 Terrace Drive
St. Louis, MO 63117
614–373–1410

Nannies by Nita
6605 Clayton Avenue,
  Suite 205
St. Louis, MO 63139
314–647–4717
Fee: $800 to $1,000

Peace of Mind Nanny
  and Placement
  Services
509 Olive Street, Suite
  1200
St. Louis, MO 63101
314–241–2273
Registration: $75;
  fee: $700

Play Pals Child Services,
  Inc.
HCR 7, Box 124
Branson, MO 65616
417–336–2233

Templeton Nannies, Inc.
6300 Main Street, Suite
  403
Kansas City, MO 64113
816–444–1888
Registration: $95;
  fee: $950

TLC for Kids, Inc.
7301 Tulane
St. Louis, MO 63130
314–752–5660
Registration: $50;
  fee: $400 to $850

Montana

Heartland Nannies &
  Companies
5500 Grant Creek Road
Missoula, MT 59802
406–542–0241
Registration: $135;
  fee: $1,200

Nannies Preferred
1313 Second West Hills
  Drive
Great Falls, MT 59404
406–727–9897
Registration: $50;
  fee: $495

Nebraska

Heartland Nannies
P.O. Box 1582
North Platte, NE 69101
800–336–9783;
308–532–7504
Registration: $50;
  fee: $1,000

Nannies of Nebraska,
  Inc.
125 South 4th Street,
  McMill Building
Norfolk, NE 68701
402–379–2444;
402–379–4121
Registration: $75;
  fee: $1,100

Nevada

Nanny's & Granny's
6440 West Coley
Las Vegas, NV 89102
702–364–5901
Registration: $250;
  fee: $750

Nanny Placement
  Agency
P.O. Box 1685
Reno, NV 89505
702–324–6561
Registration: $75;
  fee: $425 to $925

New Hampshire

Heaven Sent Nannies
Lakeview Condos, No.
  293
Enfield, NH 03748
603–632–4108
Registration: $75;
  fee: varies

The Nanny Solution,
  Inc.
P.O. Box 10278
Bedford, NH 03110
603–472–2719;
603–472–8494
Registration: $95;
  fee: $295 to $695

New Jersey

America's Nannies
340 West Passaic
Rochelle, NJ 07662
201–368–1444

Apple Pie
551 Valley, Suite 188
Upper Montclair, NJ
07043
800–598–3807;
201–589–3807
Registration: $25 to
$1,500

Apple Pie, Inc.
261 Mount Lucas Road
Princeton, NJ 08540
609–921–7399

At Your Service Agency
120 County Road
Tenafly, NJ 07670
202–894–5339
Fee: varies

CareQuest, Inc.
2 Broad Street, 3rd Floor
Red Bank, NJ 07701
908–842–1660
Registration: $50;
  fee: $850

A Choice Nanny
248 Columbia Turnpike
Florham Park, NJ 07728
908–780–3037

A Choice Nanny
RL 9 Barkalow Avenue
Freehold, NJ 07728
908–780–3037
Registration: $100

A Choice Nanny
27 Mountain Boulevard,
  Suite 9B
Warren, NJ 07059
908–754–9090

A Choice Nanny
637 Wyckoff Avenue
Wyckoff, NJ 07481
201–891–1722
Fee: $125 to $1,300

Family Care Necessities
57 Union Place, Suite
  212
Summitt, NJ 07901
908–273–2299

Kid Kare Agency
P.O. 7605
Shrewsbury, NJ 07702
908–747–2297
Fee: three weeks of nan-
  ny's salary

Love-N-Care, Inc.
16 Bayberry Road
Trenton, NJ 08618
800–538–1903
Registration: $75;
  fee: $1,200

Nannies Plus
615 West Mount Pleas-
ant Avenue
Livingston, NJ 07039
800–752–0078;
201–992–5800
Registration: $25;
fee: $1,500

Nannies USA East, Inc.
28 Hereford Drive
Prince Junction, NJ 08550
609–799–4556
Registration: $50;
fee: $1,300

The Nanny Source, Inc.
415 Route 10
Randolph, NJ 07869
201–328–1619

Neighborhood Nannies,
Inc.
205 Haddon Avenue
Haddonfield, NJ 08033
609–795–5833
Registration: $125;
fee: 20 percent of nan-
ny's annual salary

New York

Adele Poston/Park
Avenue
Bonfield Domestic
Agencies

16th East 79th Street
New York, NY 10021
212–879–7474
Fee: 30 percent of nan-
ny's annual salary

British Nanny Service
4595 Chestnut Ridge
Road, No. 1
Amhearst, NY 14228
716–877–0726

Care Finders, Inc.
1 Grove Street, Suite 112
Pittsfield, NY 14534
716–381–4840
Fee: $975 to $1,600

A Choice Nanny
130 57th Street, Suite 4E
New York, NY 10019
212–246–KIDS

A Choice Nanny
681 Lexington Avenue
New York, NY 10022
212–246–5437

Nannies by Daphne
P.O. Box 4505
Ithaca, NY 14850
607–277–NANI
Registration: $50;
fee: $850

Nannies Plus of New
  York
575 North Underhill
Syosset, NY 11791
516–496–4955

Nanny Today
264 East Broadway
New York, NY 10002
212–777–3915

Nanny's
21 Seventh Avenue
  South
New York, NY 10014
212–366–6312

A New England Nanny,
  Ltd.
2 Strawtown Road
West Nyack, NY 10994
914–353–4778
Registration: $75;
  fee: $475 to $975

Overseas Custom Maid
  Nanny Line, Inc.
P.O. Box 249
East Norwich, NY 11732
516–624–9191

Philadelphia Nanny Net-
  work, Inc.
145 West 67th Street,
  No. 31
New York, NY 10023

212–496–1213
Registration: $50;
  fee: $1,500

Preferred Nannies, Inc.
646 Main Street
Port Jefferson, NY 11777
800–323–1978;
516–474–4747
Fee: $1,100

Professional National In-
  stitute, Inc.
501 Fifth Avenue, Suite 908
New York, NY 10017
212–692–9510
Registration: $50;
  fee: 10 percent of nan-
  ny's annual salary

Quality Care Associates,
  Inc.
51 Purchase Street
Rye, NY 10580
914–967–8258
Fee: three times the nan-
  ny's weekly salary

Robin Kellner Agency
221 West 57th Street
New York, NY 10019
212–247–4141
Fee: $1,350

Unique Nannies
800 Wesley
Baldwin, NY 11510
516–546–5966

North Carolina

Chapel Hill Nannies,
   Inc.
Box 9243
Chapel Hill, NC 27515
919–942–9915
Registration: $50;
   fee: $950

Companion Sitter
   Services
RR 2
Winterville, NC 27909
919–338–5768

Nanny Connection
8331–202 Hempshire
   Place
Raleigh, NC 27613
919–870–1662
Registration: $100;
   fee: 10 percent of nanny's annual salary

Notre Maison, Inc.
6416 Carmel Road, Suite
   205
Charlotte, NC 28226
800–423–7895;

704–543–6240
Registration: $100

TLC Unlimited, Inc.
341–11 College Road,
   Suite 141
Wilmington, NC 28403
919–799–5132
Registration: $100;
   fee: up to 5 percent of
   nanny's salary

Ohio

Baby Sitting Register
210 Chestnut Street
Market, OH 45750
614–373–1410

Child Care Professional,
   Inc.
6576 Maderia Hills
   Drive
Cincinnati, OH 45243
513–561–4810
Registration: $75;
   fee: one month of nan-
   ny's salary or a mini-
   mum of $900

English Nannies
30 South Franklin
Chagrin Falls, OH 44022
216–247–0600
Fax: 800–733–1984

English Nannies and
  Governess, Ltd.
24301 Bryden Road
Beachwood, OH 44122
216–247–0602
Registration: $125;
  fee: $1,700

Home Management Ser-
  vice, Inc.
8070 Beechmont Avenue
Cincinnati, OH 45255
513–474–5800
Registration: $50;
  fee: $300

Housesitters
  International
Hudson, OH 44236
216–650–6428

Me and My Nannie and
  Senior Companions,
  Inc.
1660 Akron Peninsula
  Road, Suite 104
Akron, OH 44313
216–929–7040
Registration: $250;
  fee: $1,000

Nannies of Cleveland
1064 Forest
Cleveland, OH 44107
216–521–4650

Nanny and Me
486 Little Lane
Cincinnati, OH 45244
513–528–8630
Registration: $150;
  fee: $450

Victoria's Nannies, Inc.
7721 Five Miles Road
Cincinnati, OH 45230
513–232–0441
Registration: $250;
  fee: $750

Oklahoma

SilverSpoon Nanny
  Service
1601 South Van Buren
Enid, OK 73703
405–548–1099
Registration: $100;
  fee: $1,200

Oregon

Care Givers Placement
4004 S.W. Kelly Avenue
Portland, OR 97201
503–245–4814
Fee: $750

Northwest Nannies
11830 Kerry Parkway
Lake Osweld, OR 97577
503–245–5288

Oregon Nannies, Inc.
P.O. Box 5551
Eugene, OR 97405
503–343–3755
Fee: $1,400

Pennsylvania

Capable Care of Pennsyl-
   vania, Inc.
1 Executive Boulevard
Blue Bell, PA 15022
215–941–0336
Registration: $50;
   fee: not specified

Nanny Connection
1125 South Cedar
Allentown, PA 18103
610–439–1160

Nanny Network
225 South 15th Street
Philadelphia, PA 07102
215–546–3002

Nanny's
801 Hill Avenue
Reading, PA 19610
610–375–7375

Rhode Island

Cass and Company, Inc.
1 Richmond Square
Providence, RI 02906
401–792–0521
Fee: $850 to $1,500

Mother's and Newborn
   Homecare
123 Bellevue Avenue
Newport, RI 02840
401–849–2459

Mother's and Newborn
   Homecare
249 Wickerden Street
Providence, RI 02903
401–751–2229

South Carolina

Companions, Nurses &
   Nannies
2 Bow Circle
Hilton Head Island, SC
   29205
803–785–3600
Fee: varies

Nannies, Inc.
2903 Milwood Avenue
Columbia, SC 29205
800–728–7643;
803–254–9264
Registration: $200;
   fee: $500

South Dakota

Nannies with Dreams
RRI, Box 9
Claremont, SD 57432
605–294–5896
Registration: $100

Tennessee

Annie's Nannies
8566 Cordes
Germantown, TN 38139
901–755–1457

Nurturing Nannies
P.O. Box 30576
Knoxville, TN 37930
615–691–2804

TLC for Kids, Inc.
P.O. Box 50637
Nashville, TN 37205
615–297–1914
Registration: $50;
  fee; $750

Texas

Caring Nannies of San
  Antonio
P.O. Box 780063
San Antonio, TX 78278
210–666–2669
Registration: $100;
  fee: $850

The Executive Nanny
1428 Daryll Lane
Roanoke, TX 76262
817–23–NANNY
Registration: $100;
  fee: 10 percent of nan-
  ny's salary

Nanny Professionals,
  Inc.
P.O. Box 1253
Katy, TX 77492
713–392–4567
Registration: $100;
  fee: 10 percent of the
  nanny's annual salary

Nurture Care, Inc.
669 Airport Freeway,
  Suite 303
Hurst, TX 76053
817–285–8001
Registration: $150 to
  $300;
  fee: $1,200 for live-in,
  $800 for live-out

Professional Nanny of
  Dallas
12810 Hillcrest, Suite 112
Dallas, TX 75230
214–661–1296
Registration: $50;
  fee: 10 percent of the
  nanny's annual salary

Utah

AuPair Programme USA
36 South State Street,
   Suite 3000
Salt Lake City, UT 84111
801–943–7788
Registration: $175;
   fee: $3,175

Childcrest
36 South State Street,
   Suite 3000
Salt Lake City, UT 84111
801–943–5527
Fee: $1,285

Helper West
P.O. Box 944
Highland, UT 84003
801–756–8700
Fee: $1,500

Vermont

The Connection School
   for Nannies
232 Skitchwaug Trail
Springfield, VT 05156
802–885–3556
Registration: $100;
   fee: varies

Virginia

Capable Care of Vir-
   ginia, Inc.
8230 Leesburg Pike
Vienna, VA 22182
703–556–4495
Registration: $50;
   fee: $1,100

Carriage Trade Nannies
3239 Jupiter Lane Falls
Church, VA 22044–1610
703–534–1151

A Choice Nanny
1911 North Fort Myer
   Drive, No. 307
Rosslyn, VA 22209
800–296–2261
Registration: $125;
   fee: $600 to $1,200

A Choice Nanny
8230 Leesburg Pike
Vienna, VA 22182
703–827–2716
Registration: $25 to $125
   fee: $900 to $1,400

Mother's Aide, Inc.
P.O. Box 7088
Fairfax Station, VA
   22039
703–250–0757
Registration: $50;
   fee: $1,100

Nannies Poppins, Ltd.
301 Maple Avenue West,
  Suite DE
Vienna, VA 22180
703–938–0444
Fee: $975

The Nanny Connection
10628 Looking Glass
  Road
Richmond, VA 23235
804–379–9314
Registration: $65;
  fee: $490 to $750

Nanny Dimensions, Inc.
10560 Main Street, Suite
  513
Fairfax, VA·22030
703–691–0334
Registration: $50;
  fee: $1,275

A Nanny's World, Ltd.
6001 Staples Road
Richmond, VA 23228
804–262–1900
Fee: varies

New World Nannies,
  Inc.
8706 Melwood Lane
Richmond, VA 23229
804–282–6128
Registration: $50;
  fee: $400

Washington

Classic Nannies
264 H Street
Blaine, WA 98230
800–663–6128
Fee: $800

Everyone Needs a
  Nanny
800 Sleater -Ki Street
Olympia, WA 98503
206–438–6756

Judi Julin, R.N., Nanny-
  broker, Inc.
25620 Southeast 15th
  Street
Issaquah, WA 98027
206–624–1213
Fee: one month of nan-
  ny's salary

Lousann Nanny Service
P.O. Box 310
Cheney, WA 90004–0310
509–534–9052

Wisconsin

Be My Nanny
P.O. Box 8777
Madison, WI 53719
608–277–8282

Child Care Service of
  Wisconsin
P.O. Box 26943
Wauwatosa, WI 53226
414–782–4276
Registration: $50;
  fee: $800

KRS4 Kids, Inc.
P.O. Box 1434
Madison, WI 53701
608–251–5324
Registration: $40;
  fee: $900

Tender Care Nannies
  Placement Agency
19022 Wisconsin Drive
Chippewa Falls, WI
  54729
715–723–7050
Registration: $50;
  fee: $800

Mother's Helpmates offers the following pre-employment services throughout the United States:
  • Criminal Background Check
  • Driving Record Check
  • Credit Check
  • Payroll

We are now starting a Nanny Network and Support Group. For more information on any of our services call or write:

Mother's Helpmates
813 East Bloomingdale Avenue, Suite 160
Brandon, FL 33511
813–681–5183